THE FINAL ARCHIVES OF THE FÜHRERBUNKER

CASEMATE

Philadelphia & Oxford

THE FINAL ARCHIVES OF THE FÜHRERBUNKER

Berlin in 1945, the Chancellery and the Last Days of Hitler

PAUL VILLATOUX

XAVIER AIOLFI

This book is published in cooperation with and under license from Regi'Arm.
Adapted from *Les dernières archives du Bunker 23–26 avril* © Regi'Arm, 2018

Print Edition: ISBN 978-1-61200-9049
Digital Edition: ISBN 978-1-61200-9056

Design by Myriam Bell
Translated by Myriam Bell

Printed and bound in the Czech Republic by FINIDR, s.r.o.

CASEMATE PUBLISHERS (US)
Telephone (610) 853-9131
Fax (610) 853-9146
Email: casemate@casematepublishers.com
www.casematepublishers.com

CASEMATE PUBLISHERS (UK)
Telephone (01865) 241249
Email: casemate-uk@casematepublishers.co.uk
www.casematepublishers.co.uk

Note

The documents presented in this book were found in the Führerbunker on November 25, 1945 by a French public servant posted in Berlin, Capitaine Michel Leroy. Accompanied by other officers, he managed to make his way through to the underground level of the chancellery via an entrance that had not yet been condemned, and gathered these archives, last testaments of the dying Third Reich.

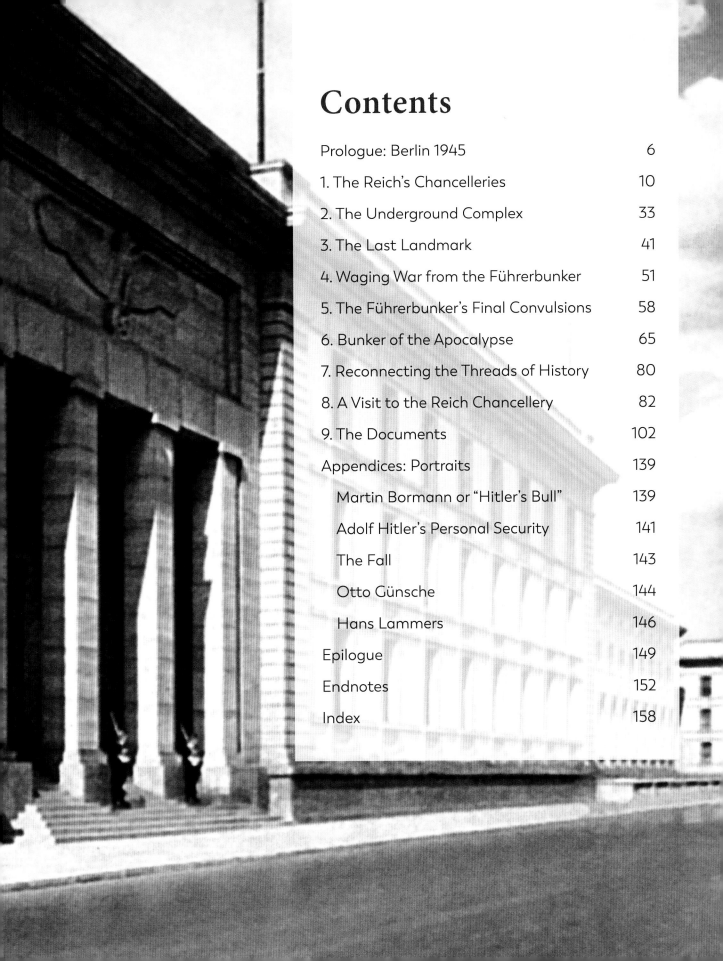

Contents

Prologue: Berlin 1945

I N THE FALL OF 1945, the center of Berlin was a landscape of ruins devastated by war. Ravaged by incessant air raids since November 1943, by spring 1945, the city was the scene of a particularly bloody assault by the Red Army, supported by artillery that, according to the most reliable sources, fired nearly 1.8 million shells. The main purpose of this barrage was to crush the morale of the Berliners who were trying to escape or hiding in the city. Street combat also inflicted heavy damage. Air raids and combat destroyed over 600,000 homes and buildings, more than a third of the city; two thirds of the center was destroyed, leaving enormous piles of rubble across most of the city. Human losses are more difficult to calculate—around

Two Red Army soldiers raising the Soviet flag over the Brandenburg Gate in May 1945. (*Library of Congress*)

60,000 soldiers, along with several tens of thousands of civilians were killed, as well as large numbers captured or wounded and thousands left homeless.

With only one in three streets cleared, most had disappeared to become narrow trenches in the rubble. Lines of refugees wandered the alleyways between buildings with roofs torn away and windows blown out. Only the Brandenburg Gate stood incongruously intact amongst the ruins.

What was left of official buildings, especially around Wilhelmstrasse, where the ministries and administration of the Reich were clustered, were a magnet for the curious victors. The chancellery and the mysterious Führerbunker—overrun by Soviet soldiers on May 2, at 15:00 and immediately searched by agents of SMERSH (the Red Army's counter-intelligence department)—attracted the most attention. Access to the bunker was forbidden for several days while the inquiry ordered by the Kremlin into Hitler's death was carried out; but the vast subterranean complex of the chancellery drew staff, civilian or military, who had been posted in the city's various zones in the summer of 1945. Many were those who, as soon as they arrived in the city, hurried to the bowels of the defeated power that had sheltered the Third Reich's leader in his last hours, searching for ghosts and mementos.

In this twilight Berlin, where three million inhabitants struggled to survive amidst the worst material difficulties, gangs of youths were spreading fear in the ruins. In the back alleys, corruption, prostitution and deals of all kinds were commonplace. Everything could be bartered, including objects or archives from the fallen regime. Those coming from the "lair of the Fascist

Above: The body of a soldier close to the remains of a vehicle in a Berlin street in May 1945. (*Library of Congress*)

Right: The cost of defeat. Two Berliners searching a dump for objects to sell or trade. (*Library of Congress*)

Beast"—as the Soviets termed the Führerbunker—were prized above others.

In the introduction to the account he left after his visit to the chancellery in November 1945, Capitaine Michel Leroy commented on the subject:

Since being set on fire by its defenders, its fall and the pillaging that followed, the Reich chancellery had received many visits. All those who filed up to see it made sure to take a souvenir with a connection, however remote, with some famous Third Reich character. Some visits and searches were official, made by the authorities of the occupying forces to recover files necessary for the trials of war criminals in Nuremberg. But many visitors behaved like vandals.

When, on the morning of Sunday November 25, 1945, Capitaine Leroy got into what remained of the chancellery by a side entrance close to the main one on the Vossstrasse, knowing how many visitors had preceded the two French officers in the last seven months, he hardly expected to lay his hands on new archive material. For him this was a simple Sunday stroll, certainly more exotic than usual, but without any purpose other than satisfying an entirely reasonable curiosity. The Reich chancellery continued to exercise the imagination and elicit questions, superstitions and rumors. The scenery remained unchanged from April 1945, whether it was the underground structures of the bunker, the emergency exit and the ventilation tower in the garden, or even the half-destroyed buildings of the chancellery...

Aerial view of the Reichskanzlei district after the end of the battle. (*Library of Congress*)

1   The Reich's Chancelleries

BERLIN, THE REICH'S CAPITAL, WAS far from being the Führer's favorite city, he was weary of its rebellious spirit and wanted to rebuild it on the model of the future Germania, which he had been dreaming about since 1925, and it was supposed to become the capital of the world by 1950. It was only fitting that the chancellery should start that process.

In 1933, the new Chancellor did not much enjoy the Radziwill Palace (formerly known as the Schulenburg Palace), at 77 Wilhelmstrasse. It had been the seat of power since Bismarck held the office in 1878, and was currently occupied by Hindenburg while the presidential palace was being renovated. The sector situated east of the Brandenburg Gate and the Tiergarten had been the official and political heart of the country since Bismarck and there was no question that Hitler should settle in any other part of town.

Adolf Hitler shaking the hand of Chancellor von Hindenburg, after being named Chancellor. (*Library of Congress*)

The Renovation of the Old Chancellery

Begun in 1739 by Carl Friedrich Richter and renovated by architect Georg Wilhelm Joachim Neumann from 1875 to 1878, the building nevertheless seemed to Hitler too old-fashioned, too small and not functional enough. The extension at 78 Wilhelmstrasse—started in 1928 under the supervision of architect Eduard Jobst Siedler—was resolutely modern, but still did not please the new Chancellor who resided there. According to him, the new wing looked like a "cigar box" or even the "administrative offices of a soap factory."[1]

May 2, 1939. Hitler addressing Berlin from the balcony of the Siedler building. (*Library of Congress*)

CHANCELLOR HITLER'S DAILY LIFE AS SEEN BY FRENCH AUTHOR ANDRÉ BEUCLER IN OCTOBER 1933

In Berlin, Adolf Hitler occupies the upper floor of the chancellery's annex, a recent construction that was added to the old historical building, which dates back to Hermann Müller. The rather severe rooms of this apartment have long been inhabited by the General Secretary and constitute a perfect example of the lodgings of a high-ranking official with no need to entertain. On the eve of revolution, the Chancellor's predecessor was putting the finishing touches to the decorating of this residence with scintillating bad taste, when he was forced to give way. Faithful to his principles of economy and simplicity, Hitler did not make any changes to the furnishings or the decoration of a place that he considers as a base, and which only his closest collaborators enter. His real home is in Munich, and it's in Munich that the Chancellor has left his private secretary, responsible for opening personal letters, sorting out photographs, dedication requests or friends' postcards.

Hitler shares his Berlin house with his chauffeur, an old comrade in arms, and militant from the early days, whose wife takes care of the house, cooking and cleaning with the help of a maid from Munich. It is also her who is in charge of the laundry and mending, as her master is not one to put up with a valet, nor any other servant. Guarded night and day by an immaculately turned out giant from his

Furniture arranged around the fireplace of the smoking room of the old chancellery after its renovation by Troost. (*Library of Congress*)

SS protection squad, the entrance door of this bourgeois interior opens directly on the chauffeur's room, a kind of waiting/living room, which continues into a rather narrow corridor at the end of which are the proper living quarters of the National Socialist Chief, his office and bedroom.

Adolf Hitler has always been an early bird. He is woken at 6:00am. At 6:30am he takes his breakfast while the phone starts ringing and his secretary and confidant Rudolf Hess, who has replaced him as head of the Party, updates him, in private, on those matters that need consideration. It's at 7:00am, or 8 at the latest, that he enters his office, located on the first floor, and starts his public life as the new Chancellor. A pile of newspapers, prepared with annotations, awaits him on his desk. According to his colleagues, the boss has a gift for, at a single glance, sorting the important from the trivial in this pile. As he examines the Reich's press, the first editors and secretaries from the ministries make their appearance, armed with their files. Remarkably, they do not hand over their paperwork and

decisions are made there and then in front of them, as they are required to deliver their reports personally. The National Socialist government, both swift and dynamic has done away with the case management system. Thus, the Chancellor's office remains generally bare, like that of a great businessman, its only ornament an inkwell. At 10:00am, meetings start, according to a rather flexible schedule kept by the State Secretary, Walther Funk, who is also in control of the national press. The petitioners are usually provincials who are forewarned the previous day by telephone, so as not to waste their time in Berlin. They almost always arrive in great numbers and are satisfied in advance that it is perfect for them: district chiefs, section commanders, syndicate association president, DAF representatives, industrialists. The National Socialist uniform dominates, but the manners, the accents, the facial features, hint at the plains of Eastern Prussia, the swamps of the Mecklenburg, the charm of Bavaria, Silesia, the Rhine. Each morning, this diverse throng submits an infinite array of items for consideration to a man who dreams of total national unity.

Entering the Chancellor's office, the first visitor raises his right arm and comes to a halt. Hitler returns the salute, approaches the newcomer with an extended hand and indicates a seat. Traditional and formal greetings have been dispensed with. The visitor addresses the Chancellor as "Mein Führer" as one would say "My General," and no longer "Herr Chancellor," or "Excellency." Indeed, the word Führer has replaced the word Chancellor in the national vocabulary, the latter having been thought to be impersonal and empty of meaning. The second group of people being seen includes businessmen, regimental comrades, old friends, journalists, minor Nazis, professional admirers, poor devils and bores, the latter come usually on foot or by bicycle from their remote provinces. But since coming to power, the Chancellor has mastered the tricky art of never making promises. He categorically refuses to accept favors and skillfully shows the door to supplicants. When it is a foreign journalist—always an event in the house—Hitler, who only speaks German, is assisted by a stenographer interpreter and takes the precaution of making the visitor sign the interview's transcript. Finally at 12:00, the diplomats are showed in. In the meantime,

Documents about the chancellery, dating from Hitler's first year as Chancellor. (*Hermann Historica*)

the Chancellor has gone to his apartment to change into a hard collar and jacket, which he will swiftly remove as soon as the last consul has left. He does not conceal from his chauffeur's wife that he cannot bear to wear the ridiculous outfit for any length of time. His favorite outfit is a town suit, a white shirt with soft collar and a plain, preferably dark, tie. The only noteworthy detail on this somber ensemble is the Party's insignia, affixed to his lapel, the swastika surmounted by an eagle.

Hitler almost always luncheons in a room adjacent to the official offices of the chancellery. It is there that he meets the ten or fifteen individuals that he has chosen that morning from the throng of visitors. But it is not unusual to find amongst these guests, a Saar workman or a blotchy militiaman with dirty fingernails and filthy boots. The conversation is usually lively, noisy: all subjects may be broached, with the exception of domestic policies. But if one wants to please the Führer and put him in a good mood, one simply asks questions about architecture, cars and music. A few of his closest friends have assured me that the sum of his knowledge and his reading make him an erudite, sparkling charmer. He has a taste for popular language, dialects, and he expresses himself in a jovial, candid and sometimes direct manner, as long as some aristocrat or pedant has not strayed into his circle of comrades and friends. Hitler does not eat meat, does not drink alcohol, does not smoke. He loves vegetables, fruit juice, soufflés, and Bavarian milk and flour recipes. It goes without saying that guests are not required to follow this diet to please their chief. They are served fish, roast meats and wine. Hitler however, does not hold large feasts and dislikes them, both because of his natural austerity and his simple appetite. He does not use his Chancellor's income, which he donates to charities, but lives solely on the income from his book, which is considerable. Since he took power, the author has seen large print runs. His book, *Mein Kampf*, is today

The main office in the old chancellery after Troost's renovations. (*Library of Congress*)

in all the libraries: earlier in the year it was flying off the shelves. His publisher sold up to 2,000 copies a day, and there is even a hardback edition that costs 43.20 Francs! Already the owner of the *Voelkischer Beobachter*, the official Reich's newspaper, Hitler is on the verge of making his fortune as a writer.

After luncheon, and if circumstances allow, the Chancellor allows himself a little nap. The afternoon is generally spent examining the political situation and acting on the decisions made. Endless conferences take place in his rooms every day. These meetings between members of the government are friendly and informal. Views are expressed freely, and discussions move cheerfully to decisions. Hitler is often required to visit East Prussia or Bavaria, two provinces close to his heart. The plane that takes him from Berlin to Königsberg or Munich is kept constantly ready for take off. These trips break the monotony of his days without interrupting the government's work: Hitler gives his orders and makes his opinions know right up to the moment he climbs into the aircraft.

He goes out little and goes to bed at midnight, never attends balls or social parties. When he is not at the theatre or the cinema, he can be found alone in his bedroom, reading. For years now, he has spent his holidays in Bavaria, in his house in Wachenfeld, Obersalzberg, which has become very popular since his victory. This rustic abode, where ministers, Party officials, farmers and photographers follow one after the other in endless succession, is under siege from morning to evening by a tight-packed, moving, screaming, tireless army of children. Mops of blond hair, decorated suspenders, red socks, blue shirts: from afar, one could swear that the Chancellor's property is a sea of wheat, poppies and cornflowers. Germany's master spends happy days there, in a loving atmosphere full of photography sessions, parades and music.

Currently, there are rumors about him of the strangest and most contradictory nature. According to some, Hitler is no longer Hitler but a head of government like any other. According to others, this rebellious little bourgeois, who has united one by one, and then in their thousands, all the rebellious bourgeois in Germany, has more power than imagination could credit: it is he, who, from his small room, runs the whole continent. According to the more "sophisticated" bourgeois, Hitler, a prisoner of his

Party, has no power; each day he faces his lieutenants, his eyes red with shed tears. Each of his speeches is modified: he concedes to Chancellor Hindenburg on the topic of expropriation; he defers to Göring who is ready, if necessary, to send the SS marching against the brown shirts. He may be animated by a sincere desire to save the nation, but beyond his loud speeches about the glory of trucks, he is unable to create and can only rant.

"Wrong!" cry the devoted. If he were to march, armed with only a stick, millions and millions of Germans would, without concern for how they would sustain themselves, immediately follow him.

Official seal of the Reich chancellery. (*Hermann Historica*)

"Hitler was born is Austria," claim the more inclined to irony, "he has a Czech accent, French hair and a British moustache. He has been tasked with leading a country whose only muse he knows is agitated and dissatisfied. Shouldn't he familiarize himself with some of the systems of government before signing even the least decree?"

"I used to know him, Hitler," says a former confidant. "I knew him at a café in Munich: he's a giant. He knows where he is going. He's like an army on the offensive! He would take care of the grains of sand on a beach in Pomerania, if he had to."

As for the Secretary of State responsible for responding to journalists, he declares that the Führer, above all else a supporter of order, has decided to favor the greater good over any private lobby, no matter what the cost. Every day God gives Germany, Hitler draws reserves of energy and passion from the people's trust in him. Everything that is done, is done well, and the newspapers of the Reich continue spreading this story across the country. So passers-by slow down when they pass the chancellery and turn their heads with reverence towards the building guarded by enraptured militiamen, where works the man, who for the last ten years, has roused a nation, called France a bastardized race and threatened the peace of Europe.[2]

Volk (people) statue, in a dining room alcove in the old chancellery. (*Library of Congress*)

His ambition was for a profound transformation of both the inside and outside of the premises, and of the decoration and furnishings. In the fall of 1933, as Hindenburg returned to his official residence, Munich architect Paul Ludwig Troost, creator of the monumental *Haus der Deutschen Kunst* (House of German Art), was named architect in charge of the renovations; his foreman was the young Albert Speer, also in charge of renovating the Siedler annex. The sudden death of Troost on January 21, 1934 did not interrupt the work, now led by Gerdy, his wife, and assisted by Leonhard Gall, who was an architect and foreman on Troost's sites in Munich. The works to modify and enlarge the building benefited from a large workforce and were swiftly completed. They included in particular the building of an air raid shelter, under the large reception room, also known as the Ambassador Room, which looked south onto the gardens.

Professor Speer became progressively more important to the Führer. After the Sielder annex, the architect was tasked to renovate the vice chancellery, the Borsig Palace, at the corner of Wilhelmstrasse and Vossstrasse, in order to shelter the Sturmabteilung's (SA) headquarters. In 1935, Speer built, at Hitler's request, a balcony on the façade of the Siedler building. The Führer wished to be able to address the people of Berlin and show himself during parades or party rallies on the Wilhelmstrasse. It was there that the Führer and Hermann Göring, chief of the Luftwaffe, would be acclaimed by a delirious population after the triumphant return from the French campaign in June 1940.

Opposite: Conference table in the Cabinet Room, Reich Chancellery, Berlin. (*Library of Congress*)

The New Chancellery

However, despite the efforts made, Hitler was not satisfied. The building, according to him, did not symbolize sufficiently the power and prestige of the regime. In truth, it appears the Führer instigated the idea of building a new and much larger chancellery in the heart of Berlin, as early as 1934–35, and that he went directly to Albert Speer. Two years later, the men had agreed on estimates, taking into account public donations and tourism to finance the work:[3] "The whole world will come to Berlin to view our edifices..." In his memoirs, the architect—promoted to General Inspector of Berlin buildings—indicated that it was on January 11, 1938 that Hitler summoned him to

Left: Color photograph of an informal scene in the apartments of the new chancellery. (*D. R.*)

Below: Meeting between Hitler and Czech president Hacha in the new Reich chancellery, on March 14, 1939. (*Library of Congress*)

officially entrust him with turning the project into a reality, within a particularly tight time frame:

I have an urgent mission for you. I will shortly be having very important discussions. And for this I will need large halls and rooms with which to impress the little potentates. For grounds, I am placing at your disposal those that overlook the Vossstrasse. Cost is not an issue. What matters is that it is quickly and sturdily built. How long do you need? Plans, models, the whole thing? For me, a year and a half or two years is too long. Can you have it done by January 10, 1939? I want to hold my next diplomatic reception in the new chancellery.[4]

On January 27, 1938, the project was given absolute priority, and nearly 5,000 workers split in day- and night-shifts were required immediately. So that the cold winter weather could not disrupt the work, special

Albert Speer showing Hermann Göring models of the future Berlin Arts Academy on June 5, 1941. (*Library of Congress*)

heating was put in place, whilst elements were constructed right across Germany and transported by train to Berlin. A remarkable organizer, Speer noted in his memoirs having ordered the tapestries before even "knowing the décor of the rooms in which they would hang." Chandeliers, monumental pieces of furniture, statues and an immense mosaic were also manufactured, whilst blocks of marble were ordered at Hitler's request for the flooring, as he wanted his visitors to "glide on the floor."

After proceeding to the preliminary demolition of the old buildings—including several former embassies of German states that had in times past been independent of Prussia (Bavaria, Saxony and Baden)—in a difficult environment, marked by hard frosts, Speer immediately started on the main work, with the completion ceremony taking place on August 2, 1938, as planned. On this occasion, Hitler made a speech in which he recalled Austria's annexation a few months earlier, and the unsuitable nature of the previous chancellery, and the "purely representative and official functions that must now be expected," thus justifying the need for a new building.

Deadlines were met, which earned Speer a gold insignia from the Party and a painting by the Führer, representing the Minoritenkirche Church in Vienna. On January 7, 1939 only a few days before the official deadline, Hitler explored in wonder the building, whose neoclassic façade stretched over 400 meters along Vossstrasse and which housed three levels of offices. Crowned by a giant eagle, wings outstretched, the western gate of the chancellery led to a courtyard of honor, and then to ceremonial stairs framed by colossal allegorical statues by Arno Breker, a friend of Speer's: the man of spirit brandishing a torch, and the keeper of the State represented with a sword, symbolizing the two pillars of the regime, the Party and the Wehrmacht. The Führer, always conscious of the effect a place could have on its visitors, just like the décor of a theater, rejoiced: "All along the route, from the entrance to the reception room, they will feel the grandeur and power of the German Empire!" Inside the building, a number of sumptuously decorated rooms inspired by Fontainebleau and Versailles—entrance hall, mosaic room, round room

Objects and documents signed by sculptor Arno Breker, dated 1939, a little after the new Reich chancellery's completion. An iron plaque, with its original case. These were the type of award given to the workers who contributed to completing this symbolic National Socialist building on time, as well as to distinguished visitors to the new chancellery. (*Hermann Historica*)

DIE NEUE REICHSKANZLEI

decorated with bas-relief, marble gallery, reception room—succeeded one another for over 220 meters. At the end of this long expanse, a monumental mahogany and marble door, six meters high, bore the initials A.H., and led to the Führer's work office—heart of the new chancellery. The room's walls were covered with immense Les Gobelins tapestries; the room itself was 27 meters long, 14.5 meters wide and over 10 meters high. Noteworthy among the characteristic artworks there were an equestrian statue of Frederick the Great, a portrait of Bismarck by Lenbach, a bust of Hindenburg, as well as a group of paintings dating from the 17th and 18th centuries.

A presentation leaflet of the new chancellery from the period. (*Private collection*)

Continued on page 26

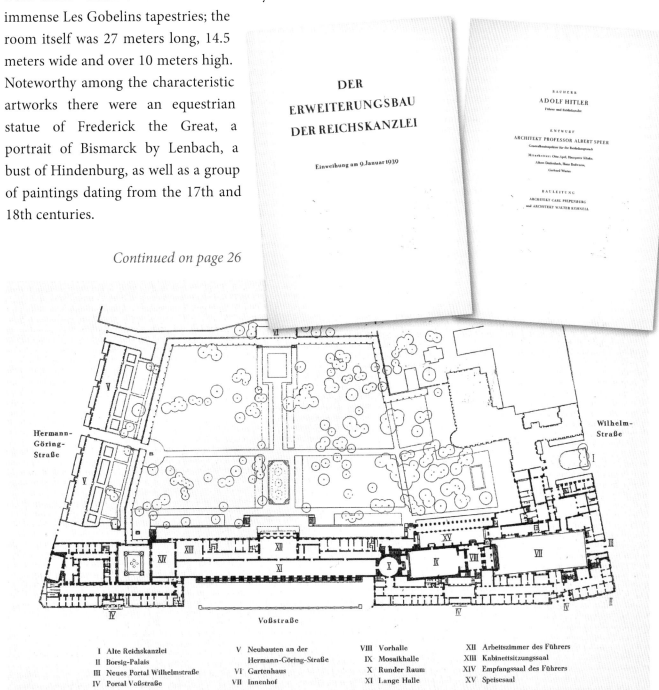

I   Alte Reichskanzlei
II   Borsig-Palais
III Neues Portal Wilhelmstraße
IV   Portal Voßstraße
V   Neubauten an der Hermann-Göring-Straße
VI   Gartenhaus
VII Innenhof
VIII Vorhalle
IX   Mosaikhalle
X   Runder Raum
XI   Lange Halle
XII Arbeitszimmer des Führers
XIII Kabinettsitzungssaal
XIV Empfangssaal des Führers
XV   Speisesaal

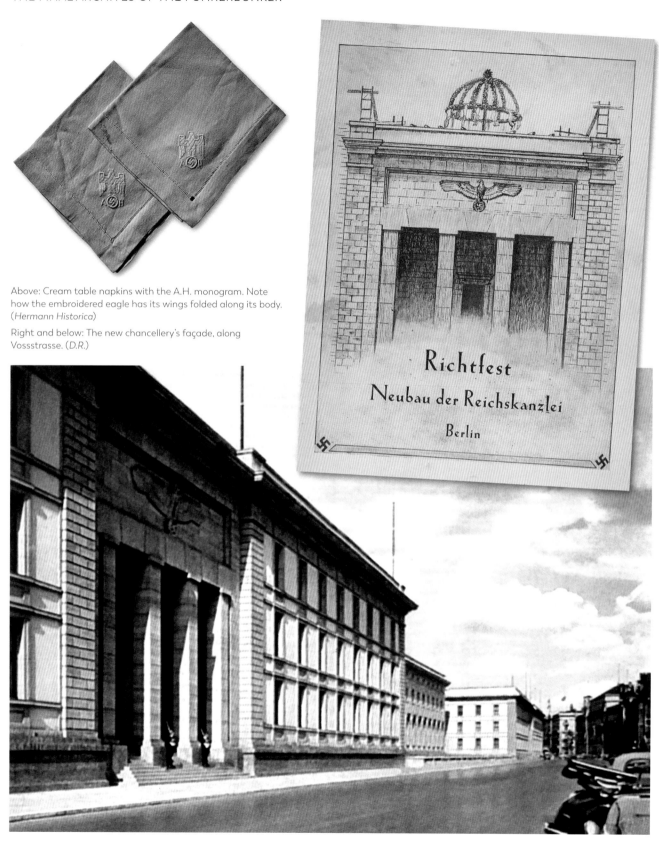

Above: Cream table napkins with the A.H. monogram. Note how the embroidered eagle has its wings folded along its body. (*Hermann Historica*)

Right and below: The new chancellery's façade, along Vossstrasse. (*D.R.*)

Richtfest

Neubau der Reichskanzlei

Berlin

Left: The opposite view of the façade of the new chancellery on Vossstrasse. (D.R.)

Below: Following Speer's perfectly planned vision, the building was full of long galleries designed to impress its visitors. (D.R.)

Above: The courtyard of the new chancellery . (*D.R.*)

Right: Miniature replicas of Arno Breker's huge allegorical statues. (*Hermann Historica*)

The monumental entrance to the Führer's office: a six-meter-tall mahogany and marble door, guarded by two members of the Leibstandarte Adolf Hitler. (*D.R.*)

On January 9, during the inauguration ceremony, in front of the workers, suppliers and artisans who helped construct the new chancellery, Hitler introduced it as the "first building of the new great German Reich which will weather the centuries." Denying any accusation of megalomania, he explained instead how his concept rested on the:

[...] coolest reflection, according to which it is only by gigantic work of this type that it is possible to make the people aware of their own conscience.

Furthermore, he added, revealing much about his frame of mind at the time:

Left: Color photograph of the sumptuous works of art that adorned the walls of the new chancellery. (*D.R.*)
Below: A panoramic view of the chancellery's dining room. (*Library of Congress*)

As a German citizen, I am today what I always was, and I do not wish to be more. My private quarters are exactly the same as they were before I came into power, and they will carry on being so. But here, I represent the German people and when I receive someone at the Reich chancellery, it is not the private man Adolf Hitler who receives, but the German nation's leader. Thus I am not the one receiving but the German people through me as an intermediary.[5]

From January 11, 1939 the guard of the chancellery was provided by the Leibstandarte Adolf Hitler (L.A.H.), an elite unit in charge of the Führer's protection. Men in parade uniforms, with white shirts and white leather equipment, therefore stood at the entrance, but also around his apartments when he was there. The distribution of

The monumental aspect of the place was accentuated by perfectly studied perspectives. (D.R.)

A view of the new chancellery's gardens, adorned with two bronze horses, designed in 1939 by one of Hitler's favorite artists, sculptor Joseph Thorak. (*D.R.*)

THE NEW CHANCELLERY, SEEN BY *LE MONDE ILLUSTRÉ*, JANUARY 21, 1939

Here in Berlin, the new palace of the Reich chancellery has been completed. A striking contrast with Berchtesgaden, where Hitler insisted on the greatest simplicity for his private residence. Here nothing has been deemed too beautiful for this huge building that must house the Führer and his collaborators.

It looks as if he wanted to replace that which he could not commandeer from the past, as other countries have, with a splendor borrowed from modern riches.

Obviously, everything here is colossal and solidly Germanic in spirit, and it is with pride that Professor Speer, the building's architect, announces that it took two and a half million bricks to build it, and that marble quarries have been exhausted.

The marble here is used everywhere, from wall coverings to parquet floors, and the Führer's office (which is only 33 meters by 15!) is completely covered with a red marble with brown veins taken from a quarry by the Lahn's banks.

This office is lit by four large bay windows and the doors, just like those of a god's temple, are made of eight kinds of precious woods, inlaid with precious silver and gold mosaics.

Tapestries and paintings have been taken from museums. Bismarck is here, and curiously Wilhelm I, in the white of a guard curassier. The rug in the reception room weighs 6,000 kg and is not the only one to measure several hundred square meters.

Finally, some figures, 200 underground parking spaces and 900 offices in the palace.

The whole building has cost several million Marks, and it is curious to note that, at the same moment that people are begging in the streets of Berlin, the Reich has denied nothing to the Führer's useless pomp.[6]

Hitler's personal desk in the new chancellery was only for show. (*D.R.*)

THE DESK DRAWER FITTINGS FROM HITLER'S OFFICE IN THE REICH CHANCELLERY

It is exceptionally rare to find a historical souvenir from the fall of Berlin, where there is absolutely no doubt as to its authenticity.

It is the case however for these two escutcheons, coming from Hitler's desk in the Reich chancellery.

The fighting in Berlin had profoundly damaged the building but did not reduce it to a smoldering pile of ash. Although partly emptied of its contents, a large proportion of the furniture remained, including the furniture from Hitler's office. Among the expensive pieces, his desk was a prized possession.

The layout of all his private spaces as well as his public ones were entrusted to the young architect Gerdy Troost, widow of the famous architect Paul Ludwig Troost.

It was she who designed the interior of Hitler's apartment in Munich, but also at the Berghof on the Obersalzberg in Berchtesgaden.

Gerdy Troost was one of Hitler's favorites because of the respect he had for her late husband, but also because of the young and pretty architect's vivacious personality.

He allowed her great freedom. Revolutionizing his office without him saying a word, keeping his used blotting papers as souvenirs, even making him change his tie for one of her deceased husband's.

Thus, it was Gerdy Troost who was placed in charge of choosing his furniture, including the desk whose door fittings are presented here.

The Russian soldiers joyfully pillaged the chancellery, but often sought more "consumable" items than historic souvenirs. In this way they emptied many a binder to

The Führer's office was at the heart of the new Reich chancellery. Its walls were a dark red marble, with ebony wood frames. The floor was also made of marble, while the ceiling was of rosewood. (D.R.)

I the undersigned Alfred de Jaeger, First Grand Prix de Rome, Artistic Advisor of the Commanding General in Germany, herby certify that these attached escutcheons come from the Führer Hitler's desk in the Reich chancellery in Berlin, they were taken in my presence (desk escutcheons, right-hand drawer).

Alfred de Jaeger is far from unknown.

He won the first prize at the École des Beaux Arts in Roubaix and Tourcoing, then first prize at the École Nationale des Arts Décoratifs de Paris in 1933. Jaeger was a student of Paul Niclausse (1879–1958), Henri Bouchard (1875–1960), Charles Despiau (1874–1946) and Henri Dropsy (1885–1969), all masters.

He won the First Grand Prix de Rome in medal engraving in 1935 with his piece *La Légende et l'Histoire*.

Artistic Advisor to General Pierre Koenig, Commander in Chief in Germany (1944–1949), it was on this occasion that he wrote the certification for these escutcheons. He was later General Secretary of the Conseil Supérieur d'Architecture et d'Urbanisme en Zone Française d'Occupation, in Germany (1945–1950), and Director des Ateliers d'Art Français (1944–1949), he died in 1992.

recover the binder itself rather than the documents it contained!

The few foreign officials who were allowed in the chancellery to bring back a memento of the war, made rather different choices, as these two fittings attest. The beneficiary is unknown, but the attestation that accompanies them is exceptional.

A quick comparison between photographs of the desk during the regime and the one from the desk today kept in the Berlin Museum, allows us to confirm that these are the original fittings and they are still missing to this day.

Beautiful chairs and tables, along with gilded bronze sconces and chandeliers gave the new chancellery's great gallery a solemn and harmonious character. (*D.R.*)

the guards was described by SS Hauptsturmführer Wilhelm Mohnke, who detailed the organization:

> The L.A.H. has established honor guard posts at the entrance of Vossstrasse (2) and in the great hall in front of the work office (2). The internal posts are at the entrance of the Führer's apartment (1), at the side entrance of the great gallery (1) and at the entrance of the cupola room (1). External posts can be found at the back of the garden (2) and in front of the garages (2). The Army's guard regiment has placed honor guard posts at the former chancellery (2), at the Vossstrasse Gate (4) and at the presidential chancellery. The SA-Standarte Feldhernhalle has honor guard posts (2) under SA command, in the inner passage leading to the chancellery (1) and on Vossstrasse.[7]

Whenever the Führer left Berlin a team went with him at all times, although two messengers remained in his quarters at the chancellery.

With the work barely finished, Hitler was already thinking of an even larger building, the Zentrale des Reichs, the Germania chancellery for which Speer was already working on plans and models. The immense building was to surpass everything that had ever been built up until now: from the entrance to the Führer's office, the diplomats would have to walk some 500 meters to get there.[8]

2 The Underground Complex

FROM 1935, EACH MINISTRY WAS equipped with an underground air raid shelter, or Luftschutzbunker, at a greater or lesser depth. In some cases, they were former cellars that were refurbished or reinforced, in others they were new concrete buildings. Of course, the Reich's chancelleries were no exception.

During the works undertaken at the existing chancellery, architect Leonhard Gall submitted plans for a large reception hall, which could serve as a ballroom in the new extension.

The Outer Bunker or Luftschutzbunker

This new room allowed him to construct an air raid shelter underneath, the foundations of which were more than five meters underground and which could be accessed from the cellars. Once signed off, the project was handed to Hochtief AG, a company that specialized in this kind of work, and who would then be contracted to work on most of the Führer's shelters in his various residences, including the complex underground system at the Berghof.

Completed by the end of 1936, and costing an estimated 250,000 Reichsmark, this Luftschutzbunker occupied more than 300 square meters, comprised of 12 ten-meter-square rooms located on each side of a twelve-meter-long corridor. Designed to withstand air raids, its ceiling was 1.6 meters thick—twice as thick as the neighboring Air Ministry's shelter—and its walls were 1.3 meters thick. Given the internal bulkheads were only 50 centimeters thick, it had an interior height of 3.08 meters, which was absolutely remarkable for a building of this kind. Furthermore, the bunker had

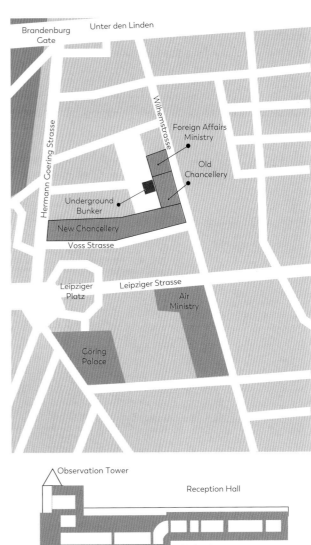

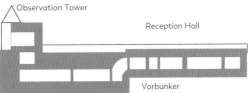

An Enigma machine, identical to those present in the Führerbunker. (*Hermann Historica*)

two entrances, one to the north, the other on the roof terrace of the dining room, to which access was controlled. When he was present in the Reich's capital, Hitler occupied the north side of the building, only a few meters away from the shelter.

The first emergency drills started in the autumn of 1937. It was in this context that detailed regulations concerning the three buildings at 77 and 78 Wilhelmstrasse and no. 1 Vossstrasse, were drawn up. Staff and residents of the last two buildings were invited to use substitute shelters, and only the chancellery's staff at no. 77 were allowed to use the shelter under the great reception hall. Its first proper use probably took place in August 1940, during the first RAF raids on Berlin.

It was only after the construction of the Führerbunker that the Luftschutzbunker of the former chancellery was officially christened Vorbunker or outer bunker. An opening was then created in the middle of the wall bordering the gardens, in order to connect the two structures via a right-angled staircase, bracketed by airtight armored doors, capable of resisting a gas attack.

General Adelbert Schulz meeting Hitler at one of his headquarters. (*Library of Congress*)

The Führerbunker

Over 1,000 complex underground networks were built by the regime to resist the bombings, a large proportion of which were in the Berlin area. Some were much more robust than the Vorbunker and were fitted with suitable, modern wartime communication equipment. For all this, Hitler spent little time in the Reich's capital and, due to his obsession with secrecy, frequently travelled in a Junkers Ju-52 or in his armored, Flak-equipped train, the Führersonderzug, first christened *Amerika*, then *Brandenburg* when the United States joined the war.

His personal involvement in the conduct of operations also necessitated that he move his general headquarters closer to the conflict in temporary wooden shelters and command bunkers fitted out for him and his staff. In order to deceive the enemy, only a handful of the dozen or so buildings of this type were actually used, the principal one being the *Wolfsschanze* (the Wolf's Lair), in the forest east of Rastenburg in East Prussia, and intermittently the *Werwolf* in Vinnytsia, Ukraine. The designation "Wolf" refers to his pre-war code name, Adolf meaning "noble wolf" in Old High German. Even if, during the day, Hitler and his generals occupied wooden barracks, the Führer inevitably returned to an underground bunker for the night, even in the early stages of the conflict, when no threat requiring this sort of precaution existed. One of his private secretaries, Christa Schröder wrote in the summer of 1942:

One of the rare known photographs to be taken in the Führerbunker, an unusual practice as the Führer, here shaking hands with Admiral Dönitz, had forbidden any pictures being taken inside the building. (*D.R.*)

> Whilst all of us were happy not to sleep in the bunker any longer, Hitler refused obstinately to leave his. We tried to explain to him that this termite lifestyle was unhygienic, he pretended that he was unable to sleep in barracks because they were sound boxes, and he spent the remaining two years of the war buried in his shelter, from which he only emerged to take a few breaths of fresh air. Whilst we had all been subject to blood circulation troubles and headaches when we slept in the confined air of the bunkers, he seemed very much at ease in this artificial atmosphere.[9]

From 1942, with the increase in British air raids on the Reich's capital, Speer recommended the building of a new shelter under the gardens of the chancellery, of

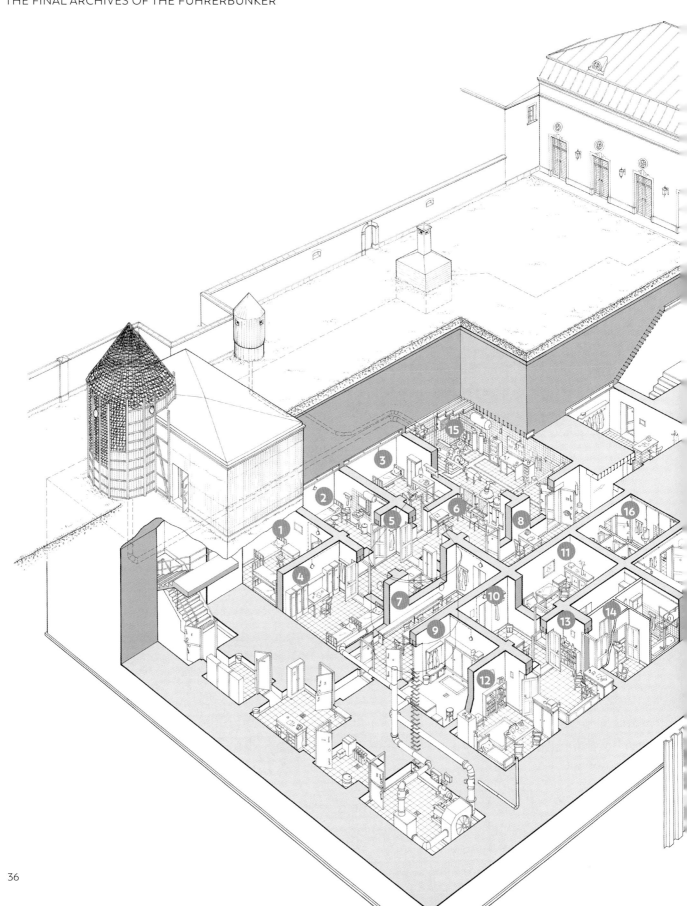

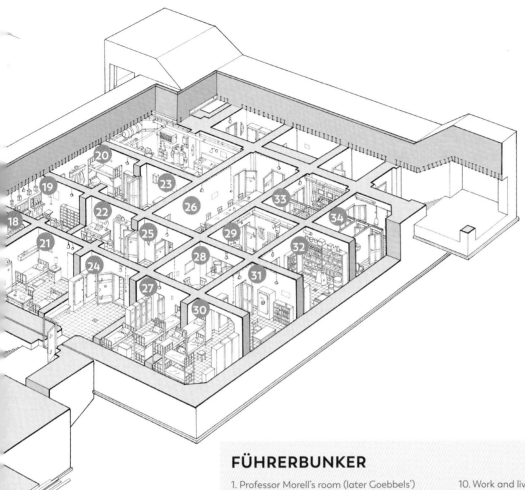

ROBERT M. JURGA

FÜHRERBUNKER

1. Professor Morell's room (later Goebbels')
2. Medical room (Dr. Sturmpfegger)
3. Service room (staff bedroom), later Martin Bormann's office.
4. Orderly dormitory (Ungel)
5. Staff restroom
6. Teletypewriters and telephones
7. Meeting room
8. Waiting corridor
9. Storeroom
10. Work and living space
11. Eva Braun's bedroom
12. Adolf Hitler's bedroom
13. Work and living space
14. Eva Braun's bathroom
15. Ventilation and filtration engine room
16. Toilets
17. Technical area for electrical equipment and the pump for waste water

VORBUNKER

18. Office
19. Former meeting room
20. Dormitories with bunk beds
21. Ordinance
22. Secretary
23. Guards' room
24. Former airtight chamber
25. Waiting room
26. Dining room
27. Dormitory with bunk beds
28. Waiting room
29. Kitchens
30. Dormitories with bunk beds
31. Treasury
32. Back kitchen
33. Bathroom and showers
34. Toilets

HITLER IN BERLIN, NOVEMBER–DECEMBER 1944

Traudl Junge, nee Gertraud Humps, was Hitler's private secretary from 1942 to 1945. (*D.R.*)

From the end of November until mid-December 1944, Hitler, who was recovering from an operation on one of his vocal cords, was still living—at least during the day—in his private apartments at the former chancellery. Life in the chancellery at this particular time was perfectly described by one of his secretaries, Traudl Junge:

I had never stayed in Berlin for an extended period with Hitler and his whole military staff. For the first time since the beginning of the war, the headquarters had been transferred to the heart of Germany in Berlin. For me, the immense complex of the Reich chancellery, framed by the former Hermann-Göring Strasse, the Vossstrasse and the Wilhelmstrasse, remained a veritable maze. I knew Hitler's apartment in the former palace on Wilhelmstrasse, but the rooms were quiet and empty, like a town house whose owners have retired to the country.

Meanwhile a few bombs had fallen here too, and the old building showed a lot of damage. It was an old and curious building, that even the transformations wrought by Hitler had never managed to make practical and fit for purpose. There was a quantity of stairs at the front and at the back, and a surprising number of entrances and their lobbies, which made accessibility difficult for important people when they were needed urgently.

On the first floor were Hitler's library and his office, his bedroom and Eva Braun's apartment. There was also a large conference room, a beautiful room which Hitler said he had rescued from falling apart. "The old man—that was what he called Hindenburg—received me in this room when he named me Reich Chancellor. 'Walk along the walls, Hitler' he said in a deep voice. 'The floor won't hold much longer.' I think the building would have slowly collapsed because nothing had ever been repaired." Hitler had then got two new ceilings installed, but a bomb had fallen precisely on that empty room and it had not been restored. This floor could be accessed from three different stairs.

Directly opposite Hitler's office door, a few steps led to a long corridor which opened on the rooms of his entourage. The first, at the foot of a few steps, was called the stairs room. It was at that time our meeting room, a waiting room for the aide-de-camp, and sometimes also a bedroom for an unexpected guest.

In the next room was Schaub, then Dr. Otto Dietrich, Press Chief, then came the room that was meant for Sepp Dietrich but was in fact now occupied by aide-de-camp Bormann, and finally there was the permanent office of Gruppenführer Albrecht, the Berlin aide-de-camp.

The corridor turned a corner towards the rooms dedicated to Morell, Colonel von Below, General Burgdorf and Professor Hoffmann. On the ground floor, the rooms were laid out in a similar fashion. There was Intendent Kannenberg's office, a small rustic room used as a staff dining room, a medical room and a bathroom. The cook and the maid resided downstairs, where the laundry and ironing rooms were also found.

Under Hitler's private apartments were the reception halls. Even with fewer rugs, furniture and precious paintings, the enormous lobby was a pleasant room, that was however never used. What was called the lounge was accessed via a small antechamber. On its right was the "Ladies Lounge," on its left was a cinema and concert room. There, three large, beautiful doors led directly onto the Chancellery's park. The "Winter Garden" was the most beautiful space in the whole building. It was a very long structure, semi-circular at one end, many high windows and doors opening onto the park. It is true that the name garden did not apply anymore, as the pretty plants and flowers that used to be there had disappeared a long time ago. In the circular part of the room, there were two round tables at which breakfast was taken. It was there that Hitler held his more mundane meetings when he did not need a large staff, in the latter case using the vast office in the new chancellery. These long, deserted spaces were suddenly coming to life again.[10]

dimensions comparable to those of the Vorbunker, but at a greater depth of 15 meters underground and with the increased protection of 4 meter-thick reinforced concrete walls. This proposition finally received the Führer's approval on January 18, 1943, as the Luftwaffe was on the point of losing the battle in the skies above Berlin. The project was code-named B-207 and the work was entrusted to architect Carl Piepenburg, from the Troost practice. The construction itself was placed with multinational company Hochtief AG once more, but also with Philipp Holzmann AG, for a total cost of 1,350,000 Reichsmark. The two companies drew on forced labor, notably *Ostarbeiter* "East workers."

The usable area of the new shelter, later referred to as the Führerbunker, was meant to be similar to that of the Vorbunker, that is 380 square meters, the level difference in height between the two being 2.5 meters. He kept the general layout, from the first bunker, of a large central corridor, divided into three parts and leading to a total of 22 rooms. Due to the thickness of the walls, these were even smaller than the ones in the Vorbunker and none were more than 10 meters square. The foundations were dug 12 meters deep in order to stabilize the ground, representing more than 8,000 cubic meters of excavated soil. As the work took place below the water table, pumps were installed to sanitize the seepage water, whilst sheet piling surrounded the site to stabilize the whole thing.

The concrete ceiling, beneath two meters of protective soil, was four meters thick as were the outer walls. A French specialist on the history of bunkers, Patrick Fleuridas, wrote in a well-documented study of the subject:

Murals discovered in 1990 on the walls of the garage adjacent to the Führerbunker. They were painted by a chauffeur and depicted among other things, idealized SS figures, the Reich's eagle and the ideal family.

The inner height is 3 meters and we can estimate that the apron is a minimum of 1.3 meters. Forty-four steps climb from the emergency exit to reach the fresh air of the chancellery's gardens. A 8.93 × 7.37 × 4.88 meters high slab (measurements taken by the Soviets in June 1946). Nearby, a five meter-high conical turret, in reinforced concrete with three low doors and rifle slits. Contrary to what many plans show, there are no links with the building below. It is a simple observation shelter for external defense, accessible from the gardens by an armored door. A second turret with identical functions remains unfinished.[11]

The shell of the structure was completed by the end of October 1944, a month before Hitler's first visit on November 20, when he was forced to leave the *Wolfsschanze* as a result of the Russian advance in East Prussia. Arriving by train in the dead of night to keep his arrival in the capital secret, he then requested for the place to be reinforced with an extra one-meter-thick concrete bomb-proof slab (*Zerschellschicht*), but this addition never saw the light of day. By that time the gray paint in the rooms and the rust colored paneling in the corridors were barely dry and, as the builders were unable to plaster them, the place remained permanently cool. A 60kw diesel generator was used for heating and lighting and a 20-meter-deep Artesian well ensured a water supply. The ventilation system made a constant and nagging buzzing noise, and a microphone hidden under a ventilation cover transmitted outside sounds.

During his first proper extended stay in Berlin since the Soviet advance, from November 20 until December 11, 1944, furniture, paintings and tapestries no longer adorned the rooms of the new chancellery having been stashed in the underground complex as protection from air raids. Although the venue for the two, long daily conferences—the first from 2:00 to 3:00pm, the second, dealing with the latest developments, in the evening and which the Führer still attended with his general staff—was usually his imposing office, it was not unusual for them to be relocated to the small conference room of the Führerbunker during air raids.

3 The Last Landmark

T HE FÜHRERBUNKER, LOCATED UNDER THE Chancellery of the Third Reich, was the spot from which the last act of a regime—dying certainly, but whose control remained focused in the hands of its creator Adolf Hitler, surrounded by his remaining followers—was played out.

From January 1945, a Reich whose fate, despite initial predictions that it would last ten centuries, was intimately linked to its creator, began to crumble. Berlin, symbolic city of Germany's unity, was the place he chose to die, amidst a scenario made all the more theatrical by the fact that it took place behind closed doors, in an atmosphere of *Götterdämmerung*.

On March 11, 1945, Hitler was given an update on the situation in the 9th Army's HQ, in Bad Saarow, in what was to be his last trip outside the German capital.

Entering the Bunker

The last German offensive in the Ardennes, Operation *Herbstnebel* (Autumn Mist), launched on December 16, 1944 ended in failure. This gamble, ordered by Hitler, granted the German army a brief respite from the inexorable advance of the Allied troops on the western front. However, it proved insufficient to shatter British and American morale, as Hitler had hoped it would, allowing him to concentrate on the Soviet threat. The situation took a dramatic turn from January 12, 1945, as the Red Army regularly made advances of between 50 and 70 km a day, on a front stretching from East Prussia to southern Poland.

On January 16, having quit the hubbub of his headquarters west of Ziegenberg, Hitler arrived on his special train—departing from Bad Nauheim for Grünewald station—returning to his suite in the new chancellery on board a heavy vehicle. It was against the advice of his generals and his entourage that he decided to move to the Reich's capital, never to leave it again. Initially, the Führer took up residence in his old quarters in the former chancellery, where, in case of an air raid warning, he could swiftly take refuge in the underground complex. His apartment there was modest, with the only luxuries being a private bathroom, a bedroom and an office decorated with a portrait of Frederick the Great by Anton Graff in an oval frame, a painting which followed the Führer to all his headquarters. Christa Schröder strikingly described these rooms:

Christa Schröder was, between 1933 and 1945, one of Hitler's secretaries. (*D.R.*)

> Hitler occupied a very narrow room where there was only space enough for a small desk, a small uncomfortable sofa, a table and three armchairs. This room was cold and unpleasant. On the left there was a bathroom, and on the right the bedroom, also reduced to the size of a prison cell. The office was completely taken over by a painting representing Frederick the Great. It always gave the impression that the old "Fritz" was severely judging you with his wide gaze. The narrowness of the room—we had to move the armchairs every time someone wanted to pass through—and its atmosphere literally paralyzed my reflexes and thoughts.[12]

The Führer's rooms were separated from the other rooms by the central corridor, the floor of which was covered in a red carpet. There was a guards' room, a telephone switchboard, a generator, an infirmary and office/bedrooms reserved for Hitler's closest friends and collaborators.

Two entrances remained in use to access the underground complex. The first was located under the reception room and opened on a narrow staircase leading to the cellars; the second one—considered an emergency exit—was accessed via the concrete turret in the gardens. Steel doors opened on to a spiral staircase, 37 steps that led directly to the Führerbunker. Telephone operator Rochus Misch described with precision the maze that he had to go through from the first entrance, as he wrote about taking up his function at the end of January 1945.

I was in charge of the switchboard, making sure that everything was working fine... I called Hermann Gretz, a postal technician, he was to explain to me how the switchboard, which was located underground, worked. He was available. We first took the cellars of the former chancellery, passing through the entrance that was close to my bedroom, on the side of the aides-de-camp wing and the Führer's apartments. We then had to go down several steps,[13] pass by the staff kitchen, the cloakroom for Hitler's small reception room, the toilets, cross a corridor which leads to a cellar nicknamed Jannenberg Alley, pass through an airtight, armored door before finding ourselves in a rather narrow room which had another two similar doors. They were open. The door in front led to the Foreign Affairs Ministry's garden, adjoining the chancellery's. The door on the left led to the concrete underground complex built for Hitler. I felt like I was in a maze. Gretz went in front. Once we had passed through that second door, we were in what Gretz called the Vorbunker, the pre-bunker or top floor of the bunker. We walked fast, without meeting anyone. We had crossed the 12-meter-long central corridor quickly. I barely had time to glance at the small side rooms that were on both sides of the corridor. At the end of it, another armored door stood open. Gretz walked forwards. Two airtight chambers, a few steps. There we are. The place is austere. The furnishing sparse and the lighting crude. The air is damp... The Führer's bunker is truly nothing special. It gives the impression of somewhere stunted, almost miserable with its empty concrete walls. Everything looks ridiculously small compared to the huge and very safe *Flachbunkers* (flat bunkers) built for civilians. The rooms are tiny, cells of three by four meters at most. To the right as one enters is the water supply for the toilets and bathrooms.

Opposite, in a space as large as two rooms, the machine room, with its ventilation system, its lights and water pumps powered by a generator. Next to this was a room of a similar size, Gretz shows me a teletypewriter, a cylinder typewriter and the switchboard... In the central aisle, barely two meters away, a heavy metal door, also open. I understand that it is an ultimate protection in case of a gas attack. Behind it are the Führer's rooms. There are five of them. A bedroom for him and another for Eva Braun. A bathroom, a small antechamber that opens onto the corridor and gives access to Hitler's office, in which a bureau, a small sofa, a table and two armchairs have been set up. That is all. Opposite, in a room on the other side of the corridor I notice Willy Arndt, Hitler's valet. He is here to arrange a few things and to make sure that he does not need anything. We leave. The journey to get back to the chancellery's ground floor takes one to two minutes at the most. Outside, in the gardens, spades and picks litter the ground next to two huge concrete blocks, an observation tower and an emergency exit from the Führer's bunker.[14]

The Final Set-up of the Führerbunker

The place was defended by guards from Adolf Hitler's close protection units, who controlled the entrances and exits. Each visitor had to present a pass, go through strict controls, leave their weapons and be accompanied by a guard to the complex's entrance. SS Oberscharführer Heinz Hantschack remembered that the SS-Sonderkommando I of the Führerbegleitkommando:

> Consisted of 14 men... each member... carried a pass with photograph, inside a red cover stamped with a golden national eagle. To enter the Führerbunker, one needed a second *Ausweis* in a black cover adorned with the SS runes. Inside was inscribed: "The carrier of this *Ausweis* is permitted to enter the Führer's apartments and the chancellery."... Guard duty alternated, sometimes day,[15] sometimes night. One of the orderlies patrolled in the garden of the chancellery, another would be found at the exit of the bunker opening onto the garden, where the concrete tower sheltered the ventilation shaft. More could be found in the doorways and corridors of the bunker, and another in the Führer's apartment.

The date at which Hitler and his entourage moved to the Führerbunker for good remains uncertain. According to Goebbels' diary, the Führer, who had left his apartments at the former chancellery, systematically spent his nights in the underground complex when he returned to Berlin, in order to protect himself from the air raids that took place daily. During the day, he occasionally went out, in particular to walk his dog Blondi in the gardens of the chancellery. Heinz Hantschack wrote:

> There were a lot of craters left by bombs in the chancellery's garden. The water reservoir for firefighting had been hit several times and had been repaired by twenty or so Russian prisoners of war, who had dug there under the surveillance of a single guard. The Chief used to walk there with Blondi. I was surprised by the limited security measures. An attack against the Führer would have been possible. I still remember how the entrance on Hermann-Göring Strasse, which opened straight onto the chancellery gardens, was hit by the bombing. At 15:00 precisely, the Chief used to go outside with his dog Blondi.[16]

According to Heinz Linge, Hitler's valet, the final move only took place between mid-February and mid-March, following the explosion of incendiary bombs in the chancellery area. On February 3, over a thousand allied B-17 bombers dropped 2,265 tons of bombs and pounded the ministries district, whilst a second massive raid against Berlin took place on February 26, launched by 1,135 bombers. Christa Schröder testified:

One of Hitler's last public appearances, photographed here on his way to a ceremony to award the Iron Cross to members of the Hitler Youth, in the gardens of the Chancellery on March 21, 1945. This photograph was autographed by Artur Axmann, who can be seen on the left. Between him and Hitler, Hermann Fegelein can be seen—he would be executed several days later for treason—and faithful Julius Schaub. On the right is General Burgdorf. (*D.R.*)

Regularly, around 11:00 pm the alarm sounded. Hitler never stayed in bed during the air raids on Berlin. He was anxious at the idea of a bomb hitting the bunker sideways and ripping a side wall apart. As the building was surrounded by ground water, he feared everyone would drown in the shelter. So, when the enemy bombers neared, he would get up, get dressed and even took care to shave. He never stayed alone in his apartment but would come to join us in the small hall. Hitler liked to take his time at dinner, which usually took place around 9:00 or 10:00 in the evening. For the duration of the meal, our radio reproduced the monotonous call of the police's special transmitter. During a raid Hitler was entirely focused on the news the radio gave of the latest attacks' development. We were at his side then, unmoving and listening out for explosions which the chancellery's neighborhood was never free from. The day after the attack of February 3, 1945 for example, 58 explosive bombs had fallen on our neighborhood. Each time one of these crashed close to the bunker, its whole mass moved. We had the impression that it literally rested on the underground water. When, due to the building shaking, the lights flickered, Hitler's voice would rise like something out of a dream: "This time, the bomb could have hit us." His face would be pale then, lines tense and his glance would move from one to another of us, full of worry. Clearly Hitler was scared. After the attacks, he would ask for reports on the damages caused. He would read them in silence, without ever commenting. Then he would retire in his bedroom to read a memoir or rest a little, so as to be ready for the night conference.[17] This last meeting of the day took place after midnight and often lasted until dawn. Then it was the usual tea, stroking the dogs, a bit of sleep until the air raid warning that always lasted until lunch. Hitler would then convene the afternoon meeting, and the same obsessive pattern would begin again.

Only the inner circle of his entourage, made up of those loyal to the end, lived close to him, in the underground complex: his valet Obersturmbannführer-SS Heinz Linge, his military attaché Obersturmbannführer-SS Otto Günsche, Kampfkommandant of the Reich chancellery, Brigadeführer Wilhelm Mohnke, his aide-de-camp Julius Schaub, his four secretaries Johanna Wolf, Gerda Christian, Christa Schröder and Traudl Junge, his nurse Erna Flegel, his chauffeur Obersturmbannführer Erich Kempka, his Viennese cook and dietician Constanze Manziarly, switchboard operator Rochus Misch, the electrician in charge of the electric equipment in his quarters Johannes Hentschel, as well as members of his private guard (among them

Johanna Wolf and Gerda Christian, two of Hitler's four secretaries. Johanna Wolf started in 1929, whilst Gerda Christian was hired in 1937. (D. R.)

Johann Rattenhuber), servants and technicians, and not forgetting his dog Blondi. The cellars of the chancellery were used as a maternity ward, a hospital for the wounded and for the Leibstandarte garrison. The number of people in this confined space increased day by day.

Amongst the regime's dignitaries, Hitler's personal physician, Theodor Morell, stayed in the room opposite the Führer's apartments. Martin Bormann, head of the Party's chancellery, also had his office there, and his own telephone exchange.[18] Despite her lover's recommendations—he wanted her to remain safe in Bavaria—Eva Braun came to Berlin during March 1945, while the Berlin-Tempelhof aerodrome was still in use. According to Colonel von Below, a witness, "She adapted completely to the atmosphere of the bunker, dressing with care and taste, remaining an example to us all in her attitude, and never showing any sign of weakness."[19] Finally, Hitler surrounded himself with a certain number of superior officers: Hans Krebs, the Heer's Deputy Chief of Staff, who replaced Guderian with whom Hitler had a violent altercation on March 28, Hermann Fegelein, Liaison Officer of Reichsführer SS Himmler, Nicolaus von Below, Liaison Officer of the Luftwaffe, Hans-Erich Voss, Liaison Officer of the Kriegsmarine, and Walter Hewel, Ribbentrop's liaison in the bunker.

THE CHANCELLERY'S UNDERGROUND COMPLEX IN JANUARY 1945, AS WITNESSED BY ARMIN LEHMANN

Armin Lehmann, a member of the Hitler Youth, was a messenger in the Führerbunker during the Battle of Berlin. His description of the underground complex is particularly precise and detailed.

Hitler entered the Führerbunker, the strange underground world which would witness the final agony of the Third Reich. The members of his staff and generals who appreciated this confined existence were few, but the Führer seemed perfectly acclimatized to it. More and more often, since events had turned to his disadvantage, he avoided daylight and preferred to direct his battles from a series of bunkers. A bad omen, the Führerbunker was the thirteenth structure of this kind that he had occupied. It was a strange upside-down world, where messenger boys, secretaries and servants gave the affectionate name of "der Chef" (the boss) to the tyrant responsible for the death of millions of people. The man who had plunged Europe in chaos and was, here, a good, fatherly boss, who loved to play with his dog...

The bunker, in reality wasn't. It was more an air raid shelter designed to provide a temporary refuge, even if it was better protected, more complex and spacious than a normal shelter. There was no sophisticated telecommunication center, nothing but a small switchboard entrusted to an SS sergeant, Rochus Misch, and a radio whose functioning depended on an antenna suspended above the bunker by a gas balloon. Towards the end, Hitler asked couriers to carry his messages to the Party's chancellery on the opposite side of Wilhelmstrasse, where the radio equipment could communicate with the Navy and the Party. However, this improved shelter was still called a bunker. The Führer had at his disposal in the Berlin area other underground complexes, more robust and equipped with modern communication systems and more appropriate to leading a war. Joseph Goebbels had a luxuriously fitted bunker in his Kaiser Information Ministry—the Wilhelm-Platz. The chief of the Reich chancellery, and Hitler's private secretary, Martin Bormann, benefited from a reinforced air raid shelter in the basement of the Party's chancellery. There was a vast complex of bunkers in Zossen, 35 km south, reserved for the Oberkommando der Wehrmacht, the Reich military high command. Superior officers asked him ceaselessly to move there. Commander-in-chief of the Air Force, Hermann Göring, was making use of the Luftwaffe's two bunkers, one located in Berlin itself, the other near the capital, in the aerodrome of Gatow. However, following the von Stauffenberg conspiracy, Hitler did not trust his superior officers; and after the repeated failures of the Luftwaffe, he saw Göring as a kind of buffoon. Consequently, he preferred the security of the modest shelter guarded by the L.A.H.

To tell the truth, there were two bunkers under the chancellery... The first bunker was just below ground, and everyone knew it as the Vorbunker, or upper bunker. Simple and rectangular, it was built around a room barely larger than a corridor, flanked on each side with a dozen rooms where could be found the kitchens, larders and the rooms for Hitler's servants and aides. This room was mostly known as the *Gemeinschaftsraum* (the common room), or sometimes as the canteen's corridor, or even dining room. When they were not left bare, the walls were painted gray or brown. The ceilings were low and the lighting weak and oppressive...

The corridor was mostly used by the subordinates, who rarely ventured in the bottom bunker, but it was a place lively with chat and gossip when guards and servants took a break between shifts. The loyalty of most of the men working in the Führerbunker went all the way back to Hitler's rise to power. Often, they would talk of the good old days in Munich, and of their stays in the mountain retreat of Berchtesgaden. On the left as one entered were the kitchen and scullery of the dietician Constance Manziarly. This 20-something Austrian woman prepared the strictly vegetarian meals of the Führer and often dined alone with him. On the right were bedrooms and quarters. They were empty in this month of January, but they would soon welcome Magda Goebbels and her six children and the corridor would become their playground.

Outside the corridor, a door gave onto a concrete stairway. At the foot of the steps were more guards from the F.B.K. (Führerbegleitkommando). An airtight door opened onto the lower bunker (whilst this was the true Führerbunker, the staff spoke of the two bunkers as if they were one and the same).

The lower bunker was 15 meters or more below the chancellery's gardens. Its reinforced concrete walls were at least two meters thick and the ceiling, also of reinforced concrete, was over four meters deep: it was covered with tons of alluvial sand, designed to absorb the impact of bombs and other explosives. The rooms of the Führerbunker had the same proportions as that of the upper bunker and were laid out just as simply. Water seeped through the walls in places, as the consolidation work had only been recently finished.

There was a large central corridor in this bunker as well. The first part was used as a *Vorzimmerlage*, an antechamber (sometimes called *Warteraum*, waiting room, or *Durchgang*, passage). The antechamber in question was the only "public" part of the bottom bunker. It was there that the visitors waited to be received by the Führer. The floor was covered in a red carpet; elegant straight-back chairs had been brought from the chancellery, and paintings hung on the walls, all contributing to give the place a civilized air. During the next three months, the Nazi Party's high dignitaries and generals would pass there to meet Hitler. Usually they were welcomed straight away with a *teewagen* (a tea trolley), loaded with fresh sandwiches (a kind of toast called *Aufschnitt*) prepared by Manziarly. The toilets, reserved for the guests, were impeccably clean, just like the ones in Hitler's private apartments.

In the gardens of the Reich chancellery, Hitler is reviewing members of the Hitler Youth who have just been decorated with the Iron Cross for their bravery. To his left is *Reichsjugendführer* (Leader of the Reich Youth) Artur Axmann. (*D.R.*)

At the end of the waiting room was a wall, with a door opening onto a similar sized room with a large central table. Each day in this conference room, Hitler assembled his generals to review the military situation. There was so little room that they all had to stand up, sometimes for hours at a time, in a suffocating heat. To the discomfiture, Hitler added angry questions: Why did his armies not counter-attack the Russian forces? The answer was simple: these armies no longer existed. But no one had the courage to admit it in front of him, and a map spread out on the table represented the situation on the ground.

Honor Badge of the Hitler Youth. (*Hermann Historica*)

On the right of the corridor could be found a half dozen rooms, the generator supplying light and ventilation, the small switchboard and Hitler's private physician, Dr. Theodor Morell's medical office. Hitler and Martin Bormann's secretaries sometimes used these rooms, sometimes working in a small living room, sometimes piling up between the treatment room and Rochus Misch's switchboard. The Führer's secretaries typed on special large characters typewriters, which allowed him to read without glasses.

On the left, was Hitler's private domain. His underground apartments contrasted cruelly with the elegance of the former Reich chancellery. A living room or antechamber was accessed via the corridor, measuring no more than three by four meters, and furnished with a sofa, a low table and three chairs. The most important documents were placed in a large case, like the thick A4 appointment diary. Then came the office, just as small and sparsely furnished, apart from the painting of Frederick the Great. Contemplating this portrait gave the Führer much comfort, he sometimes admired it by candlelight. In the bedroom, there was a single bed only. From his dining room and office, he had access to a tiny bathroom, then a bedroom/living room occupied by his mistress, Eva Braun. This room was dominated by the sturdy oak dressing table that Albert Speer had made for her in 1938. The initials E.B. were engraved in a four-leaf clover pattern.

At the far end of the corridor/conference room was a second antechamber, which was nothing more than a concrete cage, with even less furniture. There were two stairways there. The first led to an unfinished concrete tower, erected above the chancellery's gardens. The second, with its four steep concrete levels led to the emergency exit above ground, which ended in a horrible bunker guarded by men of the F.B.K. The large steel door was dominated by a small canopy opening onto the chancellery's gardens. The pillbox was entirely covered with thick *Zeltplanen* (tent canvas).

Next to the door, a kind of paddock allowed Hitler to come out at night to walk his female German Shepherd, Blondi. He said that it was the thing that relaxed him the most. And Goebbels wrote one day, with a certain malice, that Blondi must have been the only living being who truly loved the Führer.

Thus was the stage where Hitler would lead his final battle, this most mundane background where the man who had caused havoc in Europe was going to perish in the flames of eternal damnation.[20]

4 | Waging War from the Führerbunker

THE IMAGE OF HITLER COMMANDING his armies from a concrete sarcophagus under the Reich chancellery is no fantasy. It corresponds perfectly to the way he lived from the beginning of the war, which combined confinement and ascetism.

In this inhospitable hole, with its confined air, the walls were permanently seeping, and the ventilation created an over-pressurization that gave terrible headaches. German historian Joachim Fest even talks of an "[...] intolerable stench, a mixture of exhaust gas from the diesel engines, latrine smells and sweat. [...] Oily puddles stagnated in several of the corridors leading to the bunker; for a while drinking water had to be rationed."[21]

From 1942, Hitler had the discussions he had with his military chiefs on war operations transcribed. (*Library of Congress*)

THE FINAL ARCHIVES OF THE FÜHRERBUNKER

There was, according to Goebbels, an atmosphere of desolation, the tight space and artificial light creating a stressful climate. Transmissions to the outside world were made through a tiny telephone exchange with a telex, with no secure lines or reliable signal.

Hitler, War Chief

It was however, in this steel and concrete sarcophagus that for several months Hitler continued waging a war and communicating his orders to his generals. But his physical and psychological state seemed to deteriorate along with the military situation in Germany. Exhausted by intellectual overexertion, he walked with difficulty, hunched and prey to an incessant trembling in the left arm. Most of the tales of his last weeks inside the Führerbunker mention a man at times absent, at times chatty, sometimes showing signs of struggling to follow a conversation and proving himself less and less able to assume his supreme commanding role, this despite recuperative injections from doctor Morell, which were part of his daily routine in the bunker. In his memoirs, Speer described Hitler in his Führerbunker, as almost senile, waxy skinned, taking hesitant steps, speaking in a shaky voice, his uniform stained with food. However, eyewitness testimony of others who were around him during this period are much less severe. Obersturmbannführer Buttler, an officer of the Leibstandarte Division, explained that for his part:

> When I found myself sitting in front of Hitler, on April 22, towards noon, he did not give the impression of a wreck. Yes, his left arm and hand shook, but contrarily to many witnesses, he did not give me the impression of a physical wreck. He was speaking clearly and precisely and his description of the military situation corresponded to the facts, at least for the part of the front that I knew. He knew exactly where each unit was.[22]

Richard Schulze, who knew him closely and saw him daily, was more measured, saying:

> He looked tired, older. He was hunched: Schenck, his physician in his last days, compared him to Atlas bending under the weight of the sky. Above all, he was an overworked man, overloaded with worries who took a lot of medicines to keep his stamina up. His physical state was indisputably mediocre, but he remained in control of all his faculties. His intellectual qualities were not affected, his decision power either, which obviously does not mean that all his decisions were good ones.[23]

In his memoirs, Rochus Misch assured us that his authority remained intact in the Führerbunker:

Hitler seems tired certainly, sometimes on the edge, but we wondered between ourselves how he wasn't worse given the circumstances. At times, he even appeared surprisingly calm. Air raid warnings, bombs and a defeat becoming gradually more obvious by the day day never seemed to affect his authority. The reins of power remained firmly in his hands. They all came to see him. All remained the Chief's subordinates, and his alone.[24]

Martin Bormann (front right) was one of Hitler's closest advisors. Unknown to Hitler until 1933, he climbed to the very top of the Third Reich's hierarchy. (D.R.)

The important decisions were still made during the two long, daily staff meetings, which from the beginning of the conflict, had been the basis of the work done by the Oberkommando der Wehrmacht (O.K.W. or Armed Forces High Command) in the war and the linchpin of military command. Generalfeldmarschall Wilhelm Keitel, Commander in Chief of the O.K.W. whose headquarters was located in Berlin-Dahlem, southwest of the city, could be seen in the Führerbunker almost daily. General Alfred Jodl and Oberkommando des Heeres (O.K.H.) Chief of Staff, General Hans Krebs were for their parts forced an endless back and forth between the conference room in the Führerbunker, and their respective headquarters in the vast air raid shelter complex Maybach I and II, located 35 km outside Berlin in the town of Zossen-Wünsdorf.

These meetings generally began with a report, Hitler asking for an account of the situation from Jodl, Chief of Operations, in Keitel's presence, in front of large 2.5 × 1.5 m maps. The map room in the Führerbunker, judged too narrow, was soon abandoned and the meetings now took place in the central corridor. The first, which usually took place around noon, was little by little moved to the afternoon, whilst the second one, the "small" conference, which dealt with the latest developments, and in the past took place at 22:00, now often took place after midnight as the Führer adopted a more nocturnal lifestyle.[25] Decisions and all conversations held by the participants were recorded by the stenographic service. The latter comprised of eight members, who answered, in terms of administration and discipline, to Martin Bormann. They worked in teams of two, the transcription being done in three copies by typewriter, one for Hitler, the other for Scherff, whilst the remaining one was stored in the stenographic service's safe to be used as a working copy.

Regular attendees included, apart from Hitler, his aide-de-camp, Keitel, Jodl and Krebs, representatives of the Luftwaffe, Kriegsmarine and the SS and the military historiographer Walter Scherff. Martin Bormann and Ernst Kaltenbrunner, the Reich's Chief of Security, now also regularly attended the meetings. Bormann's role at the Führer's side became more and more important, as was attested by witnesses. Rochus Misch commented:

The proximity of Martin Bormann to the Führer, his apparently increasing influence on him during these last months aroused a few caustic comments... Rudolf Hess' former right-hand man, now become Hitler's "private secretary" gave the impression of being nothing but the faithful interpreter of his boss' instructions. Never did he seem to contradict him.[26]

WAGING WAR FROM THE FÜHRERBUNKER

The Final Sorties

The Führer's confinement in the chancellery's underground complex increased as the military situation degraded. From early February, he spent long hours contemplating the model of Linz, his childhood town, which was made at his request by Speer and brought by truck from the south of Germany, before being rebuilt in a corner of the bunker. Journalist André Besson perfectly described the surreal atmosphere in the bunker in this early spring of 1945:

> Everyone was playing the game and adapted to his strange habits and his aberrant lifestyle. The concept of day and night no longer existed for anyone. All that mattered was the timetable of the Führer, who only managed three hours of sleep a day. Constantly sleep-deprived, his aides-de-camp, his secretaries tried to overcome their own exhaustion with stimulants so as to remain awake and answer his requests. As in the days of Wehrmacht's enormous successes, the walls of the bunker were covered in huge maps on which little colored flags were moved around, representing the elite units currently engaged in battle.[27]

On March 3, Hitler left the capital for a few days on board his private train to briefly visit a post on the front, near Frankfurt an der Oder. Eight days later, he travelled by car to the rear area of the 9th Army in Bad Saarow, some 80 km away from the chancellery, in what would be his last trip out of Berlin. He attended a situation update at the command post of General Busse's corps, then received officers from the Berlin and Döberitz Infantry Divisions. At this point, 9th Army provided Berlin's primary defense.

The Battle for Berlin from the Bunker

Successive commanders on the Eastern Front, Guderian and then Krebs, were powerless in the face of the inexorable advance of the Red Army. The Soviets had around 2.5 million men, 6,500 tanks, and 42,000 artillery pieces, spread across three fronts: Marshal Rokossovsky's 2nd Belarus Front in Pomerania in the north, Marshal Zhukov's 1st Belarus Front in front of Küstrin and Frankfurt in the center, and Marshal Konev's 1st Ukraine Front in the south in Silesia, advancing on Saxony. The main effort against Berlin was entrusted to the last two, who Stalin put in competition with each other towards the end of March. On the German side, three large formations spread out from north to south, were Manteuffel's 5th Panzerarmee, Busse's 9th Army and the 4th Panzerarmee, who had between four and five times fewer resources than the enemy. From April 5, a 12th Army was improvised, composed of disparate elements from various Wehrmacht units.

Hitler however, was committed to defending Berlin—a *Festung* (fortress) since February 1st—in the hope of delivering a German Stalingrad. Since the beginning of March, command of the Berlin Defense Area, was entrusted to General Hellmuth Reymann. The city was then divided in eight defensive sectors named from A to H, with an advanced defensive line in the east using a chain of natural obstacles between the Dahme and the Alte Oder, stretching over 80 km; a belt of obstacles blocked the primary crossroads to the north and south of the city; an exterior defense perimeter that more or less followed the Berlin city boundaries, with pre-organized retreat positions; an interior defense perimeter, based on the U-Bahn, the underground railway; and finally an inner fortress, the *Zitadelle*, whose perimeter was based on the island made by the Spree and the Landwehr canal, with external bastions *Ost* and *West* around the Alexanderplatz and the Knie respectively, that encompassed the main ministries and the Reich chancellery.

A Hitler Youth commander is giving instructions for Berlin's defense before the Soviet forces' arrival. (*Library of Congress*)

At the Führer's request the defense of this strategic area was planned in detail: pre-positioning of antitank guns, mortars, Panzerfaust (antitank grenade launchers), installation of loopholes, stockpiling of Panzerschreck (rocket launchers). Interestingly, Speer states that it was the presence of a defensive structure of the type ordered at this time—a three-meter-high chimney capping the air vent—that prevented a murder plot, which aimed to release a can of toxic gas in one of the bunker's air vent towards the end of February or early March 1945.

In the bunker, the atmosphere was heavy, oppressive, as its inhabitants waited for the final confrontation. Conversations became less and less light-hearted, often taking place during grim meals beneath a mask of serene tranquility and an outward appearance of calm. Hitler was optimistic. He was more than ever reminded of Frederick the Great, often referring to the disastrous battle of Kunersdorf, and the happy outcome that followed thanks to the death of Tsarina Elizabeth of Russia. The words of the king of Prussia seemed to him, more than ever, to fit the situation: "He who sends the last battalion in the battle will win." On April 13, the news of Roosevelt's death was seen as an omen, a sign of fate, Goebbels maintaining the illusion for a time with Hitler, but in vain. The night before and under Speer's auspices, the last concert of the Berlin Philharmonic took place, where *Twilight of the Gods* was played. At the end of the show, members of the Hitler Youth offered cyanide pills to the public.

The Soviet attack, so long feared, began at dawn of April 16, preceded by strong artillery preparation. In the north, the progress of the Red Army's troops was limited thanks to Manteuffel's 5th Panzerarmee. In the south, Konev, who had crossed the Oder, managed to break through the 4th Panzerarmee. For his part, Zhukov suffered a setback, his assault stopped by a particularly ferocious German defense on the Seelow heights. The breakthrough was achieved on April 19, however, and only increased in the following hours. Berlin was now threatened both in the east by Zhukov, and in the south where Konev's troops were only a few hundred yards away from the Berliner Ring, the highway that ran around Berlin.

5 The Führerbunker's Final Convulsions

BURIED IN THE BUNKER, HITLER knew defeat was near, but did not want to leave his den. By then he was in no physical condition to disappear, weapon in hand, with the risk of being wounded and captured by the Soviets.

As the Reich's capital was being surrounded, Hitler celebrated his 56th birthday on April 20, in front of the regime's most important dignitaries, assembled one last time for a brief reception in a room of the new chancellery: Himmler, Göring, Goebbels, Speer, Bormann, Keitel, Jodl, Dönitz, Krebs, as well as a few gauleiters (Nazi Party regional leaders). The question that had been avoided for so long—that of fleeing south in order to form a hypothetical Alpine redoubt around the Obersalzberg, from which a "fanatical resistance" could be organized—was finally asked. The idea however was categorically refuted by Hitler, who expressed his desire to remain in Berlin and kill himself if necessary. He took his last walk outside and made his last public appearance in the ruins of the chancellery's gardens to congratulate and decorate members of a group of youthful defenders from the Hitler Youth, commanded by Artur Axmann. He tapped the cheeks of some, grabbed some by the shoulder and stammered a few words—"the battle of Berlin must be won"—and retired to the bunker for the last time.

The Last Followers

On the evening of April 20, while the bunker reverberated from the first shells falling on Berlin, Hitler showed a rare leniency by not opposing the departures of Himmler, Göring and a certain number of other Nazi dignitaries who wished to flee to south Germany. It was even he who, after a short conference with his staff, gave the order to move the services of the Party, state and administration to Bavaria. He also decided to reduce his personal staff. The activities of the stenographic services thus officially ended; six of the eight stenographers locked in the chancellery's bunker were evacuated by plane to Berchtesgaden. The two remaining stenographers left for the Berghof the next day where the transcripts were incinerated by order—it seems—of Rector Müller, Bormann's personal adviser. To these departures were added those of the aides-de-camp, the Führer's bodyguards, doctors, the press services and two of his four secretaries (Christa Schröder and

Johanna Wolf). A veritable procession thus left the city, this escape towards the country being later referred to ironically by the Berlin people as "the flight of the golden pheasants", in reference to the brown uniforms and the Party's dignitaries. In this way, as well as departures by road, all the planes from the Führer's squadron effected the evacuation of his staff over the next few days. This did not prevent the subterranean structures of the Reich chancellery from being overcrowded by an influx of refugees from neighboring houses. The infirmary, where almost 2,000 people were crammed, had to refuse entry to more.

The military situation deteriorated at an alarming rate. On the morning of April 21, the Soviet artillery fired on the city, already inflicting heavy damage in the town center itself. Thomas Fischer, grandson of a veteran, and author of a study of the battle for Berlin based on numerous eye-witness accounts, reported:

The support of Propaganda Minister Joseph Goebbels was essential to Hitler in order to retain his authority until the end. (*D.R.*)

In the Führerbunker, they were preparing for a long siege. The walls were hidden by cartons, full of jars, sausages, oats, various foodstuff, and drinks, piled up to the height of a man. 200,000 daily rations had been assembled. The food was meant to last several months. SS Unterscharführer Jochen Fellersmann, from the Führerbegleitkommando, testified that one of the largest Allied bombs had penetrated the ceiling of the upper part of the bunker (the east part), without exploding. It remained there in the middle of the provisions, near the kitchens and wine cellar. One had to take a wide berth to avoid it, so that those who did not mind the bomb could go and help themselves to treats... Furthermore, everyone felt very safe in the bunker, even when the vibrations from the bombs' detonations were so strong that they made dust fall from the ceiling.[28]

On the evening of April 21, even as Soviet soldiers were overrunning the Wehrmacht's underground complex in Zossen, Hitler held a final conference with his staff, the O.K.W. and the O.K.H., moving increasingly illusory armies around the maps. He placed all his hopes on a counter-offensive, designed to break through the Soviet forces to the north, by an improvised SS group under the command of General Steiner, into which he hoped to pour all available forces. With a strength of, at best, three battalions and a few tanks, this group had no chance of executing a maneuver of this scale, especially as the Reich's remaining forces only preoccupation now was to carve out a path to the west to escape the Soviets. In a fit of rage, the Führer demoted commander of the Berlin area, General Reymann, and dismissed Dr. Morell.

Resignation

For the first time on April 22, Hitler confided in his loved ones: "The war is lost! But you are mistaken if you think I will leave Berlin! I would rather shoot myself in the head!"[29] From then on he refused to give orders that were no longer obeyed. The Soviet pincer had been achieved and the Red Army was advancing towards the southwest suburbs and Potsdam. In the Führerbunker, anxiety was at an all-time high, as noted by Traudl Junge:

> Outside, it's hell at its worst. The rumbling of guns, explosions that make the earth shake have carried on all night long. Combat rages. The Wilhelmplatz is just a plowed field, the Kaiserhof Palace, a pile of stones and rubbles. Of Goebbels' Propaganda Ministry, nothing remains but a white-painted wall, like a cinema screen. Us, the bunker's prisoners, tried to gather a few pieces of information on the outcome of the battle. It must be at its peak. Were these our guns, our tanks making such a noise? No one was able to answer. Since January 16, the date when Hitler installed himself in his concrete shelter, we were prisoners of this bunker: it was our 96th day spent 15 meters underground. The double doors of the conference room remained shut. Bitter conversations were probably taking place, but we could hear nothing. Eva Braun had retired to her bedroom... The secretaries, Mrs. Gerda Christian, Ms. Krüger and I were staying in the kitchen, where Ms. Manziarly, dietician and personal cook for the Führer, was preparing his meal. We drank very strong, black coffee. Nobody thought to have lunch, though the usual time had long gone by. From time to time, we could hear raised voices, then nothing. The Führer was shouting words, but we couldn't understand what he was saying.[30]

In the afternoon, Joseph Goebbels moved into the Vorbunker, with his wife Magda and their six children. Armin Lehmann remembers that:

> [When] the six children entered the bunker, one after the other, their arrival cheered up the inhabitants of this underground world. For Hitler's secretaries, it was a kind of relief to see this small piece of humanity light up their universe. The claustrophobia and the sinister news of the last few days disappeared in front of the innocent voices and radiant smiles of these children, who had no idea of their nefarious fate. The top corridor was to become their playground. Constanze Manziarly would take a lot of pleasure in preparing sandwiches and pastries for these children. In some way, Traudl Junge played the role of governess in the absence of their mother. Magda suffered from palpitations and had retired to a bedroom in the top bunker. Dr. Stumpfegger took care of her.[31]

On the morning of April 23, as the Führer had given authorization to depart to those of his staff who wished to, the Führerbunker was increasingly cut off from the outside world. The Wehrmacht communications officers had left the place, taking with them the last military radios. Bernd Freytag von Loringhoven, General Krebs' aide-de-camp, reported:

> We had to make do with the Party's [radio], which did not work well, and used codes completely different to those of the army. We had to call Berlin Military Command to establish a radio-telephone connection with the O.K.W. The communication worked thanks to two transmitters installed on a relay tower in Berlin-Halensee and a tethered balloon, positioned at intervals above Rheinsberg. This system did not allow us to communicate directly with Wehrmacht Command. The snippets of information we received came from the O.K.W., with whom communications were poor and intermittent. Talking on this ultra-high frequency line required an intense physical effort. One had to concentrate to the extreme to manage to catch the words. Often, the communication would be interrupted in the middle of a sentence.[32]

Göring's Treason

Refusing to leave Berlin, to the point of proclaiming that he would defend the city to the last, Hitler worked with only a limited staff. He therefore asked Keitel and Jodl to go to Berchtesgaden and asked Krebs, Chief of Staff of the O.K.H., to remain. On April 23, SS Brigadeführer Monke officially became Commander in Chief of the Zitadelle's defensive sector, where the government resided. That same day, Speer, who had managed to get to Berlin on a small Fieseler Storch plane, came to make his last visit to the Führer in his bunker. The latter told him of his decision when the time came, to commit suicide by Eva Braun's side. In the early afternoon, he received a telegram from Göring asking him to delegate the Reich's direction to him, in accordance with the decree of June 29, 1941, which had designated him successor if the Führer was no longer able to govern:

> If I don't receive word from you by 22:00, I will assume that you are no longer free to act, and I will act on my own initiative.

Given to Hitler by Bormann, an old rival of the Luftwaffe's Chief, who deliberately emphasized its factious nature, the telegram barely aroused a reaction from the dictator in the first instance. Hans Baur reported that:

At the end of April 1945, Göring was starting to worry about Hitler's freedom of action, and feared being displaced by Heinrich Himmler, Martin Bormann or Joseph Goebbels. (*D.R.*)

> Hitler simply remarked that from the Berghof, Göring was not in a position to get an accurate idea of the situation.[33]

However, during the evening, when the British and American radios were transmitting information according to which Göring had started negotiations with the Allied forces, the Third Reich's chief became prey to a terrible anger. He immediately ordered Göring's arrest, stripped him of all his titles and answered his telegram, assuring him that he remained absolutely free to act. The answer specified:

> By your action, you have rendered yourself guilty of high treason against the Führer and National-Socialism. Treason is punishable by death. However, due to services rendered, the Führer will not exact the supreme punishment as long as you renounce all your functions.

THE ATMOSPHERE IN THE "FEVERISH BUNKER" ON APRIL 23, 1945 BY BERND FREYTAG VON LORINGHOVEN

From April 23, the bombardment of the city was ceaseless. In the bunker, regularly shaken by the artillery fire that hit the ministries, our state of nervousness was getting worse. The city was burning above us, but we didn't really know what was happening or what was betokened by the thumps of the approaching explosions, the shaking of concrete walls, and the dust falling from the ceilings. Putting your head outside one of the bunker's exits, one could smell the death roaming amid the fire and the smoke. None of us hid our fear any longer. In the corridors, each commented on the situation, mentioned all possible outcomes and the best way to proceed once the Russians made their way inside the bunker. Suicide seemed the obvious answer. Hitler had declared several times that he did not want to survive defeat. Each one of us contemplated the question of his or her own death in detail.

It had become the number one topic of conversation in the bunker. Was it better to take a pistol or swallow a pill of prussic acid? Shoot yourself in the jaw or in the temple?

In this tense atmosphere, discipline slackened. Rules that up until now had been rigorously respected were no longer followed. In the top bunker, people smoked in the corridors and antechambers. The chancellery's cellars contained an abundance of wines and schnapps. Security guards, secretaries and employees organized

This collapsing, burning building is evocative of the final battles that took place in the center of Berlin. (*D.R.*)

small parties in the corridor that served as dining room. Bottles were scattered everywhere. On the highest floor, Krebs, Burgdorf and Bormann had formed a triumvirate of drinkers who each day drowned their anxieties in alcohol. Krebs, just like the others, had not much else left to do, and depended completely on the rare pieces of information I could give him. Bormann could only rely on what reached him through the Party's channels. By the end the trio no longer used the bedrooms of the Vorbunker, but spent their nights slouched in armchairs in the corridor outside the Führer's apartments.

Krebs and Burgdorf had been friends since the time of the Reichswehr. In military circles, they had a reputation for being fond of the bottle. During one of their drinking parties, General Wilhelm Burgdorf, Hitler's first aide-de-camp and Chief of the Army Staff Office, lashed out at Bormann, Chief of the Party's chancellery and Hitler's Secretary, and through him at the Nazi leaders. This ardent national-socialist had accused them of having made money off the German people and recognized that he had been badly mistaken. Krebs has to play mediator before this inseparable clique took its final libation. By necessity as much as conviction, Boldt and I remained separate from this mess. Work helped us to remain clear-headed in the hysterical atmosphere of this "madhouse." We shared a room—bunk beds, two desks, two phones—off the corridor that went through the Vorbunker located under the new chancellery. General Krebs had a bed in the same room. The inhabitants of the bunker had quickly learned that I was responsible for collecting information for Krebs and Hitler. Out of caution, I had always kept my distance from the inhabitants, fearing saying something I shouldn't and being denounced. Suddenly Boldt and I had become important, almost indispensable. Worn down by anxiety and the wait, the recluses of the bunker had nothing to do but walk the corridors, looking for the latest news. Whenever we appeared, they would rush to us to ask if we had any news. Although subordinates, our value was constantly on the rise. Suddenly it seemed opportune not to ignore the military, to be friendly to them and even to make them promises.

Reichsmarschall Göring's
shoulder epaulettes.
(*Hermann Historica*)

It was thus, on the evening of the very same day, the Reichmarschall was arrested by the SS; Koller, Deputy Chief of Staff of the Luftwaffe, met the same fate a day later. At the same time, Hitler took steps to ensure the succession of the Luftwaffe's Commander in Chief. He urgently summoned General Ritter von Greim to Berlin, who was transported in a light plane piloted by the famous aviator, and committed Nazi, Hanna Reitsch, who was wounded by shrapnel during this rather dangerous mission.[34] Having named Ritter von Greim Generalfeldmarschall, he entrusted him with the command of a crumbling air force, abandoned to its own devices and whose ruins were scattered across the aerodromes that remained in German hands.

6 | Bunker of the Apocalypse

"THE CHANCELLERY HAD BECOME A small fortress in the midst of the ruins of the city." Otto Günsche's words testify to the feeling that the world was ending that gripped the remaining occupants of the Führerbunker.

Nothing remained, from this point on, of German unity. General Weidling—tasked by Hitler with the defense of a Berlin ravaged by Allied bombings and Soviet artillery—had at his disposal a disparate garrison of barely 75,000 men. Within the last ring of defenders were 300 soldiers of the Charlemagne Division, commanded by Captain Henri Fenet, who had managed to reach the capital on April 24 to wage a final battle side by side with other volunteers, Danes and Norwegians, of the SS Division Nordland, a few Spaniards from the Azul Division and a handful of the Hitlerjugend. Their mission: to stop the enemy from reaching the entrance of the Führer's bunker until the end.

On April 29, 1945, elements from the 301st Soviet Infantry Division, occupied the building at No. 8 Prinz-Albrecht-Strasse, which sheltered the R.S.H.A. (Reich Main Security Office) and the staff of the Reichführer SS. This image was taken in July 1945. (*U.S. Signal Corps*)

Out of Time

On April 25, Americans and Soviets linked up on the Elbe, at Torgau. A day later, the Red Army launched the final assault on Berlin's city center. The Germans' defense was stupefying and cost the Soviets huge losses in armored vehicles (800 tanks), targeted by the formidable Panzerfaust. The Tiergarten fell on the evening of April 26, the enemy now less than a kilometer from the chancellery, but only managing to fully clear the area the next day, April 27. The atmosphere inside the Führerbunker was surreal, as described by Traudl Junge:

We are cut off from the outside world, apart from a wireless phone line with Marshal Keitel... They met with little resistance in their march through the center of the city and were approaching Anhalt Station without slowing down. The Führer wandered around the bunker's dark rooms like a ghost, crossing corridors in silence, entering rooms. At times I wondered why he did not put an end to all this. It was clear by this point, that nothing could be salvaged...

The former Reich chancellery next to the new one, at the corner of Wilhelmstrasse and Vossstrasse, on May 4, 1945, two days after the end of the fighting. (*U.S. Signal Corps*)

Eva Braun was writing her farewell letters. All the dresses that she loved so much, her jewelry and a few valuables were sent to Munich. She too waited and suffered. Externally, she still showed the same calm resignation, the same serenity.[35]

However, on the morning of April 28, Hitler and Krebs regained confidence when they learned of the 12th Army's progress under General Wenck's command, an army that had been hastily put together a few weeks earlier. After having crossed the Halbe Forest, it reached the village of Beelitz, 20 km south of Potsdam. Bernd Freytag von Loringhoven witnessed this mad hope and the disappointment that followed:

The T-34/85 was the standard vehicle for the Soviet tank brigades during the Battle of Berlin. (*D.R.*)

The news spread like wildfire. The inhabitants of the bunker, most of them with no military knowledge whatsoever, began to regain confidence in the Führer's lucky star. I saw smiling faces asking if the news of Wenck were true. This euphoria was short-lived. Without news of Wenck for several hours, we finally heard the same message of success on the German radio. "In their attack to free Berlin, the young divisions of Wenck's army have reached the area to the south of Ferch." Some in the bunker immediately cried betrayal. If the Russians had not yet guessed it, Wenck's objective was no longer in doubt. The next day, in a communication from the O.K.W., we learned that Wenck's attacking divisions had been pushed back westwards. By evening, the news left no doubt as to his failure. This last illusion gone, the bunker plunged back into despair. With all hope finally lost, death became the new preoccupation again. Hitler had made clear his intention of ending his days. The rumor had it that he would shoot himself and Eva Braun would take poison. "We are nothing more than a morgue!" said someone, expressing the prevailing feeling... In the night of April 27 to 28, the bombardment redoubled in intensity. Within the concrete block of the Führerbunker, we could feel the vibrations of the incessant pounding of the chancellery by the Russian artillery . The Vorbunker's ceiling, much thinner, was threatening to give way under the shells. Water seeped in the Kannenberggang, holes everywhere from the projectiles. Intermittently, the makeshift light that functioned thanks to a generator, would start working again. The bunker was descending into chaos. Everywhere, dirt accumulated. The trash was no longer taken out. Mattresses were piled up any which way in the corridors. Dust and smoke came in through openings and vents.[36]

Cut Off from the World

In this end-of-the-world atmosphere, Hitler boiled with rage when he discovered on April 28 that Eva Braun's brother-in-law, Hermann Fegelein, was getting ready to flee. He had him arrested and executed on the night of April 29. In the middle of the afternoon, when Stockholm radio announced that Himmler had made contact with the British and Americans, the Führer vented his anger one last time. Shortly before midnight, Walter Wagner, registrar of Berlin, entered the bunker so as to marry Hitler and Eva Braun. The ceremony was reduced to its simplest form, in the presence of two witnesses, Goebbels and Bormann. A few hours earlier Hitler had dictated to Traudl Junge his two wills, one private, a few pages long, and the other political. In the latter, he named Admiral Dönitz as his successor, Generalfeldmarschall Schörner commander of the Wehrmacht's remaining forces, Bormann was named the new Party Chancellor and Gauleiter Hank Reichsführer SS instead of Himmler. The two documents were sent to safety outside the bunker by Colonel von Below, Heinz Lorenz and Zender, one of Martin Bormann's deputies.

The Soviets were now at the end of Wilhelmstrasse and beginning to push into Potsdamer Platz. Mohnke testified to the terror that now seized him:

> I will never forget how Hitler told me the news, that had reached him first, that the Russian tanks had managed to break through the Potsdamer Platz, only 300 meters away from us. We all thought: "Now this is it, the storming of the Reich chancellery." What else could I do but repel the Russians by counter-attacking with all the forces, gathered in haste, that were at my disposal. We not only had to defend the occupants of the Führerbunker, but also a military hospital with several hundred severely wounded and numerous civilians, above all women and children, who had taken refuge in the Reich chancellery. During the counter-attack, we managed to destroy the Russian tanks, partly in close combat.[37]

The situation became more and more desperate, so much so that Weidling, who could not guarantee the chancellery's security beyond May 1, presented a plan to leave the chancellery, which was rejected straight away by Hitler. Thomas Fischer noted that now:

Heavy blows were raining down upon the Reich chancellery, so that the ventilators had to be stopped every 15 minutes because of the fact that they sucked sulfurous fumes and lime dust into the bunker.[38]

On April 29, the Soviet troops pushed up Wilhelmstrasse and the buildings that symbolized the regime fell one by one. The combat remained fierce, Fenet and his men in particular made an impression by managing to destroy about 60 enemy tanks.

In his memoirs, Rochus Misch remembered:

It was the end. A heavy, absolute silence reigned in the bunker, a veritable concrete sarcophagus. Everyone guessed that the Führer was going to end his life in the coming hours. Every one of us wondered what fate awaited us after his death. The news coming from the last German forces still engaged was comfortless: attempts to breach the Soviet line had failed. During the day of April 29, and into the evening, small groups of men left the chancellery to try a final breakout. Little by little, the number of residents shrunk.[39]

The destruction wrought by the Soviet shelling and air raids, during the fighting on Oberwallstrasse, close to the State Opera. (*D.R.*)

The Bunker of Death

On the morning of April 30, Hitler summoned Mohnke in order to ask him how long he could hold on. The latter answered him: "24 hours my Führer, no longer!" He then called for his aide-de-camp to give him his last instructions, including those for cremating his and his wife's bodies. "The last day in the bunker was the day of the apocalypse," stated Otto Günsche. After one last meal with his immediate entourage, the Führer said his goodbyes to his remaining followers, in a surreal atmosphere perfectly described by Armin Lehmann:

The smoldering ruins of the German capital after the fighting ended. Henri Dariès, present on the ground left a vivid testimony: "It is clear that violent fighting took place here recently: their marks catch the eye everywhere. I am quite alone among these nightmarish ruins, though they are clearly still inhabited." (*D.R.*)

An SS officer came to announce that the Führer was ready to say his last farewell. The news of his imminent departure promptly went around the chancellery. A festive atmosphere had seized civilians and soldiers alike. A gramophone played music, people sang and danced. While the Führer climbed to the top bunker, the noise had become such that the phone operator, Rochus Misch, had to ask for silence. To no avail. An SS officer then ordered the revelers to calm down, but once again the request fell upon deaf ears. Hitler finally arrived at the door

of the top bunker, accompanied by the ever-present Martin Bormann. The cries and laughs were becoming deafening. Around 20 servants and guards were assembled. Hitler walked past secretaries, junior ranks, and officers and they said their goodbyes for a last time. Rare were those who remembered what he had said to them, he had simply grumbled a few platitudes. But he addressed them and freed them of their oaths before wishing them good luck. He also bade them to escape the Russians. For his part, he had no choice but to die in Berlin. He didn't want Stalin to put him on display in a museum... There was no hope left. The Führer showed no emotions. He called Bormann to inform him that he would kill himself in the afternoon, and asked his deputy officer, Otto Günsche, to take care of his cremation... During lunch, he gave each woman present a poison capsule, apologizing for having nothing better to give them.[40]

All the bunkers' occupants mentioned Eva Braun's courage and serenity as she faced her death. (D.R.)

Hitler and his wife retired to their apartments around 15:00; Linge, Hitler's valet opened the door for the last time. Straight away Günsche ordered Erich Kempka to procure 200 liters of petrol in the car park and barred the access to the private rooms of the bunker with guards from the Führer's personal detachment. A deadly silence reigned then. Günsche reported:

Hitler had given me the order to wait ten minutes, then to enter the apartment. The longest minutes of my life. I posted myself, like a sentinel, in front of the door, hand on my pistol. Almost straight away, we saw Magda Goebbels rushing towards me, as if to force her way through. Unable to stop her, I opened the door to ask Hitler for instructions. She almost shoved me out of the way to enter, but she came back out again almost immediately as the Führer had refused to listen to her, and she left, sobbing. A moment later, Axmann arrived with his aide-de-camp. This time I was firm: "Too late!" I was looking at my watch and was listening intently. There were six or seven of us waiting in front of the door.[41]

After ten minutes, although the double doors to Hitler's apartment, perfectly sound-proofed, had betrayed no sound, Günsche, Linge and Bormann entered the rooms and discovered the two bodies: Hitler's head, from which ran a trickle of blood, was looking towards the floor; his wife collapsed against him, legs folded on the sofa. The characteristic smell of cyanide—tested before on the dog, Blondi—filled the room, mixed with that of powder. Misch reported:

> At the back of the cell that we called the living room, I could see Hitler's motionless body. I didn't come in. I was six, perhaps eight meters away. Hitler was sat on the little sofa, bent over himself, near the table. Eva was near him, huddled on the sofa, her chest almost touching her knees. She was wearing a dark blue dress with white flower trimming.[42]

Berlin, after the final battle in May 1945. The center is a field of ruins as shown in this official photograph, taken by a Red Army photographer; note the Gedächtniskirche's bell tower in the background. (*Library of Congress*)

Doctor Ludwig Stumpfegger, the Führer's private surgeon, made a note of the time of death at between 15:30 and 15:40. As arranged, Linge, with Bormann's

help, wrapped Hitler's body in his brown dressing gown and then in a military blanket, to transport him with the help of six SS soldiers of his personal guard, to the chancellery's gardens. Eva Braun-Hitler's body was lifted by Bormann, then carried by Günsche and the guards outside the bunker, under heavy artillery fire. Kempka and a few guards carried petrol jerrycans, with which they doused the two corpses, which had been placed at the bottom of a crater left by a shell. The audience, composed of Bormann, Linge, Kempka, Goebbels, Rattenhuber, Müller, Hewel, Krebs, Burgdorf, Mohnke and Günsche, managed after some effort to start the fire, by throwing burning pieces of paper down. Whilst the bodies caught fire, all stood giving the Hitler salute, then quickly retired to the bunker. The cremation continued for several hours, but was not complete. Günsche took care to retrieve the Führer's two pistols, one of which, the 7.65mm, was used for the fatal shot, whilst Linge burned all the papers that lay around the private apartments of the former leader of the Third Reich.

THE FINAL ARCHIVES OF THE FÜHRERBUNKER

Fleeing the Bunker

In the underground complex of the chancellery, things had in the meantime become more casual. Drawing near the supplies, Traudl Junge heard cries and drunken laughter and stumbled upon an orgy, and later wrote:

> An erotic fever seemed to have taken hold of everyone. Everywhere, even on the dentist chair, I saw bodies entwined in languid embraces. Women had renounced all modesty and freely exhibited their private parts.[43]

Armin Lehmann also remembered:

> The gaiety, which that same morning had disrupted the Führer's farewells, had turned into a nameless debauchery. The dentist chair, which could be set in different positions, was apparently very convenient for carnal unions. Everywhere, in the basements and air-raid shelters of the chancellery, men and women were making love, a last and desperate attempt to find some comfort before the horrors that awaited them. They did not care about the elderly or the mothers and their babies, indifferent to the cries of the dying piled up at Professor Haase's, indifferent too to the bombs that were falling in the streets. Numerous SS soldiers, charged with hunting down deserters and fighting until the last, had already proved faithless. They had pillaged the chancellery's reserves: champagne, chocolates and sweets which they found attracted women.[44]

Most occupants of the bunker were by now preparing for a *Durchbrechen* (breakout), Gerda Christian recalled:

> After Hitler's death, there was a sudden slackening of the tension, which had reached unbearable heights. We started planning for our departure and it helped distract us. That night we were ready to leave, but Brigadeführer Mohnke came in to give us his orders: the breakthrough had been delayed by 24 hours.[45]

Some preferred the idea of dying in the bunker, so as not to fall into the hands of the Soviets, who had raised the Red Banner over the Reichstag at 14:30 on April 30. Indeed, the latter were refusing to negotiate, despite several tentative approaches agreed during a meeting in the Führerbunker following Hitler's death. A little after 18:00, on May 1, Goebbels therefore made his preparations with Dr. Stumpfegger to commit suicide with his family. The cremation of the eight bodies, which was only superficial, took place that evening. Burgdorf, Krebs and Müller committed suicide in turn.

The flight of the remaining followers took place at 23:00, under Mohnke's orders, in a ravaged city, amidst the wounded, the last soldiers and frightened civilians. House by house, the Red Army continued to gain ground, and were scrupulously clearing each district, each building, each shelter, each basement where terrified and exhausted inhabitants had hidden. Ten groups—composed of soldiers, women and civilians—were to break through the Soviet lines from the bunker in a north westerly direction towards Mecklenburg. The first group comprised Mohnke, Günsche, Hewel, Admiral Voss, Klingmeier as well as the Führer's secretaries and his dietician. Mohnke remembered:

I left the Reich chancellery first, by a hole in the wall, and crossed Wilhelmplatz, running towards the Kaiserhof's underground entrance. The others were following close behind. We had to be fast, in the end the Russians started shooting. Then we ran along the tracks to get through the Russian lines. This risky escape route ran through the U-Bahn tunnel that initially

The *Altes Museum* (the Old Museum), which sheltered an antique collection was heavily damaged at the end of the fighting. Note the unusual presence of a Mark I British tank, dating from World War I. (*Library of Congress*)

followed Friedrichstrasse, which ran from the Stadtmitte interchange. I took some comfort in the knowledge of the Ivans' aversion for tunnels. But the Russians were already there... From Friedrichstrasse, we took a footbridge over the Spree, avoiding the Weidendamm bridge... The groups that followed found themselves caught in the crossfire in the middle of a battle. Heavy, direct fire was raining on the Weidendamm bridge... We crossed streets lined with houses full of bullet holes and shrapnel, then continuing through ruined buildings, cellars and breaches in the walls, running from one basement to the next, the escape route quickly led us towards Invalidenstrasse, then on in the direction of Wedding, first along Chausseestrasse past Maikäfer barracks, up to a road block covered by a Russian tank. We then had to turn right, running through backyards and side streets (Bernauerstrasse) towards Brunnenstrasse all the way to Humboldthain. There, we met General Börenfänger; as if in a

May 2, 1945. Two Red Army soldiers flying the Soviet flag on the roof of the Reichstag palace in Berlin. This image became the symbol of the end of the Battle of Berlin and of the fall of the Third Reich. (*Library of Congress*)

deep calm we reached and rested in the shade of the tall Flakbunker in the Prinzenallee and then the Schultheiss-Patzenhofer brewery, where we found refuge in the cellar.[46]

Having reached a dead end, the group finally surrendered on May 2, around 21:00, some six hours after the end of the Battle of Berlin and the ceasefire agreed by General Weidling, Commander of the Berlin Defense Area.

Bormann was part of the third group, alongside Stumpfegger, Baur and Secretary of State Werner Naumann, who, after wandering in the Berlin underground, managed to reach Unter den Linden Avenue and the Weidendamm bridge. All trace of them was then lost. Long considered missing in action, the former chief of the Party's chancellery in fact died on May 2, 1945 on Invalidenstrasse, where his body, as well as Stumpfegger's, was exhumed in 1972 and formally identified in 1998.

In the chaos that was Berlin, Soviet troops systematically pillaged everything. Objects recalling the fallen regime were especially prized, like this bust of the Führer. (*Hermann Historica*)

The last occupant of the chancellery's bunker was Johannes Hentschel, Chief Electrician in charge of the machinery and the lever which could in case of emergency shut down everything and seal the armored doors. Mohnke asserts that at no point was the order given to loot or burn the bunker.

Why should I set the bunker on fire? At that point, I certainly wasn't thinking of souvenir hunters. I realized that hundreds of people in a makeshift hospital under the Reich chancellery would be lost without the water and electricity supply from the bunker! I also knew that the machinist [Johannes Hentschel] was still on duty and kept the machinery running. In any case we wouldn't have had enough petrol to do it. It was limited to the incineration, as best they could, of the corpses.[47]

Hentschel was therefore the sole German to greet the first Soviet troops to enter the bunker, ten or so women physicians, who appear to have arrived by chance, engaged in the first looting by taking some of Eva Braun's lingerie. Later on, men arrived who took Hentschel outside the bunker. Preceded by engineers, equipped with mine detectors, the Red Army soldiers secured the place before being ousted by agents of the SMERSH (Soviet counter-intelligence service), from the 1st Byelorussian front, who then forbade access during the investigation. This was above all about finding

An official silver coffee set on a tray from the new chancellery. (*Hermann Historica*)

the Führer's body. On May 5, based on a prisoner's testimony, the corpses of a man and a woman were exhumed from the chancellery's gardens. Badly burnt, the remains were kept in an East German barracks until the 1970s when they were destroyed on the K.G.B.'s orders. Nothing remained, apart from a tooth identified thanks to two dental bridges. For many months, the theory of Hitler's flight abroad gained credibility with the public and it wasn't until the British historian, Hugh Trevor-Roper, gave a press conference on November 1, 1945 that the first credible account of Hitler's last hours in the bunker, was given.

In the meantime, as soon as the SMERSH investigation was over, the bunker was systematically pillaged by the Soviets. James P. O'Donnell, information officer of the U.S. Army Signal Corps, and first western soldier to visit the complex (after bribing a Soviet soldier who was guarding the entrance), noted during his visit on July 4, 1945 that no object of value was left. He compared the place with the "Paris Market after an auction." He noticed the indescribable mess, water everywhere, traces of fire and a fetid smell.[48] He also observed however that numerous papers, books and official documents remained.

Trophy of the SS Standarte Deutschland. (*Hermann Historica*)

7 Reconnecting the Threads of History

ALL HIS LIFE, ADOLF HITLER was a lover of Richard Wagner's music. As a young student in Vienna, he knew each note of his music scores, and happily identified with his characters. Like the Dutchman from the *Flying Dutchman*, he is offered, in his last concrete-limited days of April 1945 in Berlin, a prelude of his eternal damnation.

Lurking in his lair of concrete, isolated from the world and distanced from people, Hitler, in death, turned the last moments of his regime into a legend.

Very few events in human history can boast to have been so intertwined with political plotting and morbid fascination. In rationalizing the chaos of these historical events, the Russian government not only erased all traces of them but made it near impossible to know what had really transpired.

For a long time, history had to make do with a few dates and names, the vague description of a place, a short film replayed over and over again, and a few photographs of ransacked rooms. Historians would need decades to piece together what happened, and to restore the last moments of a world that had been meticulously erased.

The concrete bunker was destroyed, a garden planted in its place, and almost everything that had escaped the flames lit by the last occupants of the bunker was secreted away by the Soviets; the remains of flesh and bones vanished, direct witnesses "re-educated" and history revised. This became an event lacking the fingerprints or physical evidence necessary to a reliable testimony.

However, history demands facts and answers and they had to be found. Reluctantly out of the ruins of the former Soviet Union, came some bits of dental debris and a piece of bone. Skeptical at first, historians went back to the original miasma which had shaken up the story of the bunker and continued to hover between hints and certainties.

As for what was the "reality," the veil that had fallen on the scene can never truly be lifted. But thanks to a movie, *Downfall*, in 2004, we were able to glimpse in a tangible form something that had, since 1945, been just a ghostly silhouette. Bruno Ganz's mastery finally gave a voice, a posture, an atmosphere and surroundings to the facts.

But it would take the fruits of two French officials' curiosity to, finally, bring form to this descent into hell.

A casket with papers from the New Reich Chancellery. An allied soldier's war souvenir. (*Hermann Historica*)

8 A Visit to the Reich Chancellery

By the end of April 1945, the Soviet army had reached the Tiergarten and the immediate vicinity of the Reich chancellery, the full name of which was the *Präsidialkanzlei des Führers und Reichskanzlers*, where Adolf Hitler and his remaining followers, hidden in the underground cellars converted into comfortable offices with armchairs, sofas, wool rugs and more, lived out the tragedy of the Third Reich's demise. Their resistance futile, the palace's defenders set fire to it to destroy official documents and deny to history the last days of the National Socialist chancellery. Everyone knew that Hitler was in the chancellery and the Soviet army

In the autumn of 1945, the city of Berlin was a desolate spectacle. Destroyed buildings and ruins were everywhere in the German capital. (*Library of Congress*)

did what it could to seize him in person or recover his body. But its efforts were not rewarded and even now, seven months later, we have not been given irrefutable proof of his death. At best, we can assume that Hitler and Eva Braun's bodies were among the charred corpses recovered in the gardens of the *Präsidialkanzlei*.

So begins the tale told in November 1945 by Capitaine Michel Leroy, of his visit to the Reich chancellery and its underground complex. The son of a railroad worker, the French officer had just celebrated his 36th birthday and owed his rank to the peculiar mission that had been assigned to him a few weeks earlier. Michel Leroy was an employee of the S.N.C.F. (French railways), which he had joined after gaining a

A photograph of Capitaine Michel Leroy and his orders signed by Général Louis Koeltz, the French government representative of the French Group for the Control Council in Berlin, and deputy to the French Commander in Chief in Germany.

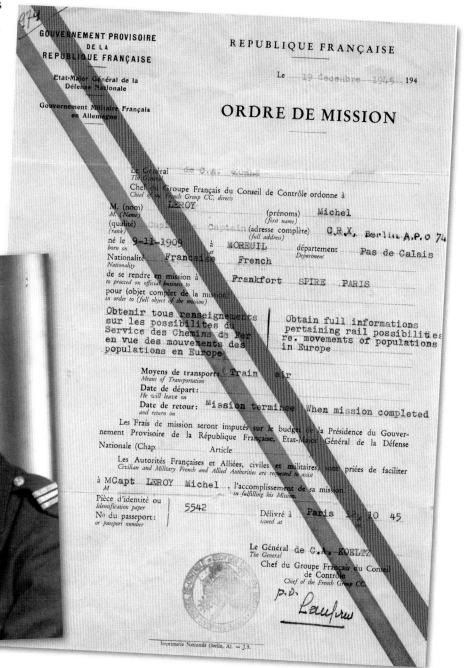

commercial engineering degree at the Université of Lille. On October 12, 1945, he was attached to the Groupe Français du Conseil de Contrôle (G.F.C.C. or French Group for the Control Council), as the permanent secretary of transports to Berlin, with a mission to "obtain any information about the capabilities of the Railway Services, given the movements of the European population."

Under the Potsdam agreement of August 2, 1945, the repatriation of German minorities had to be ensured, as they were being expelled from Czechoslovakia, Hungary, Austria and Poland. The task was gigantic as it was believed to involve fifteen million *Volkdeutsche* (Ethnic Germans). It was made all the more difficult by the fact that expulsions had already taken place covertly, and millions of people were wandering the roads wearing a distinctive colored armband. To proceed in an "orderly and humane fashion," a Combined Repatriation Executive (C.R.X.) was established by the Allies, so as to bring together representatives of the expelling countries and the occupying powers. However, it had neither the authority nor the means to avoid the humanitarian disaster which awaited these people. A French

Opposite: Two German children looking for food in the autumn of 1945. In the background, German soldiers recently freed from Soviet prison camps pass through Berlin. (*Library of Congress*)

Below: Two elderly men, one of them wearing an armband indicating his blindness, sit on a box in amidst of the ruins of Berlin, 1945. (*Library of Congress*)

zone was thus established to receive 150,000 Sudeten Germans, passing through Austria and gathering in Red Cross-approved transit camps, awaiting transfer according to the timetables established by the C.R.X.

Capitaine Leroy was then part of a team, led by Commandant Raymond Rose, which also included Jean-Jacques Meillong, Capitaine Jean (or Yvan) Wiazemsky, a Russian prince, whose family took refuge in France, and Claire Mauriac. The latter, daughter of author François Mauriac and a Red Cross ambulance driver during the war, decided once the conflict was over to leave for Berlin in order to help the thousands of wounded, destitute and refugees. The Berlin that she described to her family, "a gigantic refugee sorting machine" under Soviet control is especially striking:

> What an ugly thing is Berlin! One can barely conceive the sadness of this enormous city which does not have a single house left whole. What is a thousand times worse is the Berliners living in basements and dying of hunger...[49]

In a letter written on October 15, 1945, Claire Mauriac also gave account of the living conditions of the group to which she belonged:

> We live in a large four-storey house. A madhouse where one is never bored. On the first floor are the Belgian and French [women]. Offices and bedrooms, dining room, etc. On the second floor are the offices of the French officers. On the third floor, apartments of the Displaced Persons Division's staff. On the fourth floor, several bedrooms including mine.[50]

The devastated landscape of the German capital at the end of 1945, in the background is the Victory Column. (*Library of Congress*)

Witnesses to a devastated German capital after the Allies' victory, the French elements of the control group were naturally interested in visiting the place which had sheltered the last moments of the Nazi regime. In a letter sent to her parents on September 11, 1945, Claire Mauriac even confided:

> Yesterday I went to visit the chancellery. I saw Hitler's office, his bedroom and his shelter. I took a few pieces of marble from his office. I will go back because I would like a bigger one.[51]

So, when on November 25, 1945, after both going there in the morning, Commandant Rose and Capitaine Leroy asked Jean-Jacques Meillon, Jean Wiazemsky and Claire Mauriac to join them for a second visit, they did not hesitate in following them. They knew that they were disobeying Soviet orders, and fraudulently entering a part of history.

Equipped with electric torches, the members of the little group were perfectly aware of the layout of the place, thanks to information supplied by other colleagues having made the visit the previous Sunday. It is possible that Claire Mauriac even gave them precious information. To enter the building, they followed a circuitous and unorthodox route: a window located in a corner of Vossstrasse. They made their way through rubble, scraps of metal and broken furniture. Suddenly the light of their torches came to rest upon a hidden stairway, access to which was obstructed by a mound of debris, which they cleared away. Beyond these eight steps, another stairway led to an immense, dark room with square columns that they identified as a dining room due to the presence of a table loaded with broken crockery.

The team advanced slowly. In an adjacent room, where furniture that had been torn apart and half burned lay, Capitaine Leroy discovered a painting

Bronze eagle from the chancellery, given to the occupying British troops by a Soviet officer in 1946, and today part of an exhibition at the Imperial War Museum. (*P. Villatoux*)

A rare photograph taken by Soviet troops, of the Führer's HQ inside the bunker, which was partially burned in May 1945. (*D.R.*)

hanging crookedly, which he took and which he later learned belonged to Arthur Kannenberg, Hitler's steward. A third room revealed bronze statues, vestige of the 1936 Olympic games. Retracing their steps, the chancellery's visitors noticed a heavy steel door set in the wall of the dining room. It led to a stairway of 26 steps that they descended towards a new basement. "The atmosphere is warm, heavy, unbreathable, no air and still that burnt smell..." Noted Michel Leroy. They understood then that they had just entered the Führerbunker with its interconnected bedrooms, offices, dormitories and bathrooms. Leroy indicated that: "everything is upside down, sofas, ripped armchairs, overturned chairs, ransacked mahogany desks emptied of their drawers, which themselves had been emptied of their folders." Among this mess, worthless books and papers littered the floor.

They finally discovered a small work desk, at the very end of the complex, which they guessed was likely to be Martin Bormann's.

In the half-light of their electric torches, they started their quest. Left in a heap at the edge of a desk, documents attracted their attention. Original documents that had escaped the attentions of the many different visits which had taken place over the previous seven months. Among them, around ten telegrams of incredible historical importance, which helped understand the frame of mind of the last dignitaries of the Third Reich, as well as some of the events which took place between April 23 and 26, 1945.

A safe in the Führerbunker, broken into by Soviet soldiers. (*D.R.*)

They took the documents and shared them as souvenirs. Both Capitaine Leroy and Commandant Rose guessed the importance of these documents, which was confirmed to them when they got them translated. Both of them would write the story of their visit and keep their treasure; both of them could now help write history. Life went on and all that was left were the direct testimonies of their visit, which curiously surfaced on the market almost at the same time. On returning to France in November 1948, Michel Leroy once again took up his position in the commercial services of the S.N.C.F., where he led a brilliant career until May 1966. He died on March 6, 1980, and never made public his discovery.

Commandant Rose, whose documents now form part of the prestigious Bruno Ledoux collection, chose the pieces that related to Göring's treason, which shook the bunker in its last days. This served to illuminate and bring color to a historical moment as shocking to the bunkers' residents as it was trivial in the scope of the conflict's last days.

For his part, Capitaine Leroy chose to unearth history of the sort that isn't obvious at a glance, but requires one to decipher page after page with patience, determination, curiosity and a love of detail. This history is profoundly human, as raw as it is brutal, and plunges us into events that even Wagner would not have dreamt of.

It is a story of a life that is gone, of a moment in history, of the lessons that it forces us to learn and of the secrets we are obliged to unearth.

It allows us today to follow, page by page, amid the pervasive smell of smoke and damp, the final spasms of the last act of a dark, bloody opera.

An American officer saluting two Soviet soldiers guarding the bunker's entrance in 1945. (*Library of Congress*)

Above: Aerial view of the Tiergarten, the famous Berlin park, in 1946. (*Library of Congress*)

Below: The Brandenburg Gate as the Allies' occupation zones were being set up. (*Library of Congress*)

Left: A staged photograph of the "beast's lair." (*D.R.*)

Below left: This photo gives a good idea of the chaos that reigned in the bunker's rooms after it was looted by the Red Army. (*D.R.*)

Below right: Photographer William Vandivert, from *Life* magazine, took these photographs of the bunker after the Red Army pillaged it. Here, an American soldier holding a candle. (*D.R.*)

A Soviet soldier posing in one of the bunker's rooms. (*D.R.*)

Right and opposite: Allied troops inspecting the chancellery's gardens. The Red Army had already made its investigation and these photographs were staged for the western press. (*D.R.*)

Left: Three German women saving the few belongings that are left to them. They are walking past the Air Ministry. (*Library of Congress*)

Right: A member of the Soviet military police directing traffic in front of the Brandenburg Gate in the Soviet sector of Berlin. (*Library of Congress*)

Below: A staged Soviet propaganda photograph of a *Reichsadler* (Reich eagle) with its swastika. (*D.R.*)

Right and below: In the summer of 1945, Winston Churchill was the first non-Soviet Allied leader to visit the chancellery's site. He visited the Führerbunker, as seen in these photographs. (*Library of Congress*)

Above: Soviet soldiers assembled in front of the Brandenburg Gate on May 2, 1945. (*Library of Congress*)

Left: Of all Germany, Berlin was hit hardest in 1945. In the first weeks its inhabitants didn't have the right to leave their district. According to Soviet statistics, two weeks after the surrender, of the Berlin population of 2 million individuals, 70 percent were women, children, invalids and "citizens of independent means." (*Library of Congress*)

Opposite: The Kaiser Wilhelm Gedächtniskirche shortly after the end of the fighting. (*Library of Congress*)

Below: A rubble worker has her meal in the ruins of Berlin. (*Library of Congress*)

9   The Documents

THE DOCUMENTS RECOVERED BY CAPITAINE Leroy seem to have come straight out of hell. But they are not simply echoing the deafening sounds of the chaos whence they came; nearly 70 years later, they still retain marks from the fire to which they were subjected.

The smell that still emanates from them, stale and damp, is a striking reminder of their provenance. These documents seem to have retained a sense of history. They are a material, palpable testimony, and an irrefutable proof of the events they document. Like Ariadne's thread, they are indispensable to any who wish to plunge in the labyrinth.

These 70 documents found in Martin Bormann's office allow us to navigate the final days in the bunker. Firstly, both chronologically and in its importance, was Hermann Göring's treason.

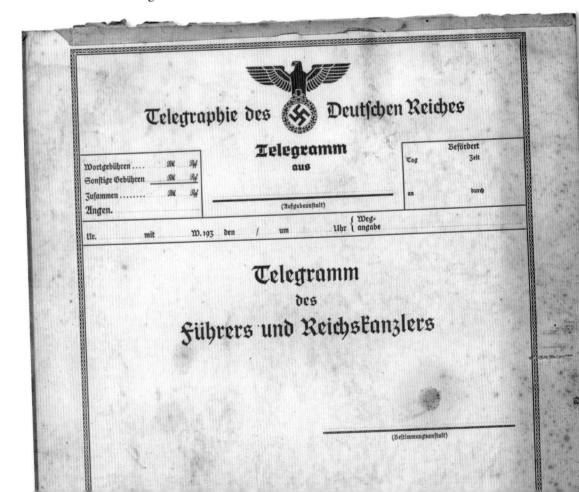

Paper used for the Führer's official telegrams sent by mail.

May God Protect You...

"... and allow you to rejoin us quickly." These are the words with which Göring ended his telegram to Adolf Hitler. So what is the truth behind the storm created by this famous telegram and Göring's "treason"? For anyone who met him in the last months of his life, and even more in his last weeks, Hitler had changed drastically. His skin was gray, he shuffled, his eyes no longer had that searing spark, one of his hands was trembling constantly. He no longer cast the heavy shadow he once had, a pale copy of the caricature that would be made of him later.

Along with these physical changes, his mentality had also completely transformed. He was now prey to furious outbursts, he no longer tried nor pretended to persuade and gave free rein to his feelings.

It was thus, on April 22, 1945, following a conference with his staff where the reality and the scale of the military situation was made obvious to him, he went into one of these terrible rages.

Official portrait of Marshal Göring at the height of his power. (*Hermann Historica*)

After a hysterical tantrum, he proclaimed his decision never to leave Berlin under any circumstances and to kill himself. Not without adding sarcastically: "if it comes to negotiating, Göring will be far better at it than me." Even in the enclosed atmosphere of the bunker, word began to spread. A general[52] told another, who repeated it to another, who told a third until the information reached the peaks of Berchtesgaden, where Hermann Göring had taken refuge in his chalet on the Obersalzberg.

In truth, these were not idle words from Hitler. In the first place, because Göring was always the one Hitler trusted when delicate discussions needed to take place bypassing the official channels. Was it because of the chivalry of the Great War fighter pilots, of whom Göring was one of the most celebrated? Or was it his flamboyant character which was better perceived abroad?

Whatever the reason, it was he who, via the Swedish Consul Raoul Nordling,[53] broached an armistice with the French troops on May 18, 1940, a month before it was finally signed.

Finally, and particularly because by the decree of June 29, 1941, following Rudolf Hess' departure for England, Hitler had named Göring as his successor in the event of a power vacuum. It was therefore entirely legitimate that Göring should be the one negotiating a capitulation as Hitler's successor, Hitler having announced that he would kill himself.

Once the news had reached him, a real storm broke in Göring's mind, with him not know what to think. The decree would only take effect when Hitler was dead, and as the latter was still alive, there was no question of taking his verbal statement literally and acting as if this were already the case. But each day counted. Neither was it possible to wait for a hypothetical announcement of Hitler's death.

Göring therefore decided to take advice. By a twist of fate, a depressed official had come to Berchtesgaden, where he owned a chalet, for his mental health—Dr. Hans Lammers. A lawyer and high German official, he was for a time Secretary of the State at the Reich chancellery. He was one of the Reich's most important officials. It was he who, among other things, was in charge of all the decrees and ordnances. In 1944, Bormann had provoked his dismissal. Hans Lammers was the man for the job, as it was he who had orgainzed the famous succession decree. This man had helped define the rights and prerogatives of the Nazi state. It could not have been planned better.

However, confronted with this problem, the oracle remained mute. He barely managed to suggest sending a telegram to Hitler to ask the question, hoping that this was the best way to go about it. If Hitler did not answer, it would mean that he was unable to, and things would be understood.

After much hesitation, Göring, full of trepidation, wrote a telegram whose every word was carefully weighed. After a first version, sent on April 23 at 00:56am, which was delayed and never reached the bunker's teletypewriters, Göring finally wrote the following message:

To the Führer. My Führer, given your decision to remain at your post in the Berlin fortress, do you approve of me taking in hand immediately the Reich's management, of me disposing of full powers, domestic and foreign, as your delegate according to the June 29, 1941 decree? If no answer reaches me by 10:00 this evening, I will consider that you are no longer free to act, that the conditions of the decree have been met and I will act to the best of my abilities in the interest of our country and people. You know the feelings I have for you at this time, the gravest hours of my life. Words cannot express them. May God protect you and allow you to rejoin us quickly. Your devoted Hermann Göring.

The telegram seized by Leroy bore the initials "F.D.R." in the margins (For Conformity) as well as the radio-transmitter's signature, which confirmed its reception for posterity. It was marked *Chefsache* (Chief's Business), which denoted a telegram personally destined to Hitler. Indeed, Hitler's immediate entourage had adopted the nickname of "Chief", and less often that of Führer, when referring to him. For safety reasons, Göring also sent explanatory telegrams to Keitel, Ribbentrop and Nicolaus von Below.[54]

Today, we know of two copies of Göring's telegram to Hitler, which both came from Bormann's desk. One sent on April 23 at 14:53 and received the same day at 15:10, came from Capitaine Leroy's archives, the other from Commandant Rose's archives.

The reception of this telegram in the Führerbunker had more impact than a Bolshevik bomb. This political bombshell was an opportunity for Bormann at a time when, more than ever, he monopolized the Führer's attention. Bormann seized the explanatory telegram addressed to von Below and rushed to show it to Hitler.

Bormann highlighted the passage where Göring demanded a reply before 22:00, claiming it was an ultimatum. The arrow found its mark and Hitler went into an appalling rage.

Göring found himself under arrest for high treason in less time than it took for the telegram to arrive, and was threatened with being stood up in front of the mountains and shot.

Dienststelle: **OB.D.L.**   FUNK   **6.OB.D.L.** stelle:

Spruch Nr.	Befördert am	193		Uhr durch
1894	Aufgenommen am **23. 4.**	19**35**	**1510**	Uhr durch
	Erhalten am	193		Uhr

Fern-Funf-Blink- **Spruch Nr. 1894** von

an

Vermerke: **DRINGENDE OFFZ.SACHE F R R   CHEFSACHE**

Absendende Stelle:	te Meldung	Ort		Tag Monat	Stunde Minuten
ROBINSON 4	Abgegangen			**23.4.**	**1453KR**
	Angekommen				
	An **KURFUERST**				

AN DEN FUEHRER.

MEIN FUEHRER,SIND SIE EINVERSTANDEN,DASS ICH,NACH IHREM ENTSCHLUSS

IM GEFECHTSSTAND DER FESTUNG BERLIN ZU VERBLEIBEN,GEMAESS IHRES

ERLASSES VOM 29.6.1941 ALS IHR STELLVERTRETER SOFORT DIE GESAMTE

FUEHRUNG DES REICHES UEBERNEHME MIT VOLLER HANDLUNGSFREIHEIT NACH

INNEN UND AUSSEN.

FALLS BIS 2200 UHR KEINE ANTWORT ERFOLGT,NEHME ICH AN,DASS SIE

IHRER HANDLUNGSFREIHEIT BERAUBT SIND.ICH WERDE DANN DIE VORAUS-

SETZUNGEN IHRES ERLASSES ALS GEGEBEN ANSEHEN UND ZUM WOHLE FUER

VOLK UND VATERLAND HANDELN.

WAS ICH IN DIESEN SCHWE STEN STUNDEN MEINES LEBENS FUER SIE

EMPFINDE,WISSEN SIE,UND ICH KANN ES DURCH WORTE NICHT AUSDRUECKEN.

GOTT SCHUETZE SIE UND LASSE SIE TROTZ ALLEM MOEGLICHST BALD HIER-

HERKOMMEN.

IHR GETREUER HERMANN GOERING.

F.D.R.

Original telegram of "Göring's treason" received at the Führerbunker on April 23, 1945 at 15:10.

Several angry responses—that put the teletypewriters ill at ease—later and Hitler finally gave up the idea to have him executed, but expelled him from the N.S.D.A.P. and fired him from his various positions. However, Bormann did not give up so easily, and tried his best to cause this one of his many rivals as much trouble as possible. The proof was found in the archives recovered by Leroy.

He started with this telegram on April 23, at 20:33, addressed to the officers of the R.S.D.[55] still in Berchtesgaden:

Reichsleiter to Bredow[56] and Frank,[57] Obersalzberg. Immediately arrest Göring's male entourage—Stop—In addition place General Köller[58] under honorable arrest. Bormann.

The copy that was preserved was in fact a draft signed by Bormann himself. The extensive marks of fire damage left on it certainly add to its chilling nature.

On April 24, at 01:25am, with nobody able to sleep under the Soviet shelling, Bormann persisted and signed a telegram, testifying to his unrivalled hatred of those in league, however remotely, with Göring. In another handwritten draft addressed to Zenger[59] of the Obersalzberg R.S.D. Service 1, he wrote:

Arrest immediately Captain Rauch,[60] Docteur Lammers' warrant officer. Store documents safely.

The radio transmitter's note in the margin of the date and time (23.4 at 20:33), as well as the handwritten initials confirm that it was sent. This order followed the one that ordered the arrest of Dr. Lammers. Bormann likely gave these instructions with great pleasure as he could not stand the man and had arranged to take his place and completely remove him from state affairs.

The reference to the "documents" to be stored "safely," concerned the decree of June 29, 1941, the original of which Göring kept with him in a tin.

Then, another telegram from Bormann's hand, dated April 25, that showed the determined and unrelenting way he sought new evidence of this high treason.

Reichsleiter to Dr. Frank – Klopfer[61] Obersalzberg. By order of the Führer: 1) Send a telegram if you have found the proposed radio address planned by Göring. If so, send a copy here by plane. 2) Have you found other documentation indicating high treason. If so, send copies here too as soon as possible.

This confirms the existence of communication by air with Berlin until the very end of the regime. The radio transmitter's note in the margin of the date and time (25.4 at 06:29), as well as the handwritten initials confirm that it was sent.

While Bormann was refusing to release his prey, Death was waiting patiently in the bunker. Although a few days earlier he declared himself lost, Hitler had one last flurry and decided on a final roll of the dice.

Hitler's Last Military Order

And so, in what would be his very last staff conference, on April 25, he declared to the assembly:

> To my eyes, there is no doubt that the battle has reached its peak. If it is really true that in San Francisco, differences are emerging between the Allies—and this will be the case—a real transformation could occur if I can land a blow on the Bolshevik giant. Then, others might finally be convinced that only one entity can contain the Bolshevik colossus: me and the Party and the German State... If destiny decides otherwise, I will disappear from the political world scene, a dishonored and obscure fugitive.

He therefore decided to send one last order to his troops, to gather a last formation to launch a final battle. The only proof of this today is an A4 telegram. Dated April 25, 1945 at 06:23, sent by Adolf Hitler to Reichsleiter Bormann, to be sent to the concerned parties. It also shows how the Nazi machine had not lost anything of its administrative rigor, even so close to the abyss.

A large red stamp indicates: *Chefsache! Nur durch Offizier*! (Chief business, to be transmitted by officer only). The official note, handwritten by Bormann in the left corner, says "Gegen Rückgabe an Z" (return to Z).

The text is a snapshot of history, its vain illusions and chimeric hopes.

> 1) The O.K.W. is responsible to me for the conduct of operations.
> 2) It will act according to my instructions, which I will transmit via Army Chief of Staff, General der Infanterie Krebs, who is by my side.
> > A) In the southern sector with help from Staff B (Generalleutnant Winter). South and Center Army Group. South West HQ. South East HQ. West HQ.
> > B) In the northern sector. DIRECTLY. Norway Defense Sector (Army Commandment no. 20), Denmark Defense Sector, North West HQ. 12th Army.

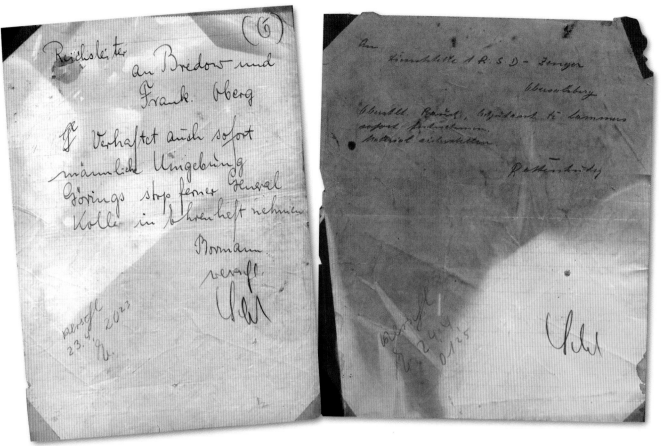

Army Group Vistula with the 9th Army. East Prussia Army. Kurland Army Group.

3) For now, the general direction of the operations, under Admiral Dönitz will not come into effect.

4) The main objective for the O.K.W. will be, by means of an all-out attack from the North West, South West and South, to urgently and by all means necessary establish a communications link with Berlin and thus bring about a victory in the Battle for Berlin.

5) The Army's HQ Group and the General Inspector for armored forces are now under the command of the Army Chief of Staff. The Army's Quartermaster General will be under direct the direct command of the Wehrmacht's Quartermaster General, and will receive its instructions from him.

6) Orders for the O.K.L. will follow.

Two fire-damaged handwritten telegrams. Both concern the Göring affair. On the left is the original in Bormann's hand addressed to the Obersalzberg services. On the right, a telegram sent by Johann Rattenhuber, Chief of the R.S.D., to the same services.

Hitler was still oscillating between oblivion and hope as he sent these last orders. The two first points show his state of mind towards his army. They reflect his absolute distrust and his fear of being betrayed.

Fernschreibstelle

WRKF	001483
Fernschreibname	Laufende Nr.

Angenommen Aufgenommen		Befördert:		Gegen Rückgabe
Datum: 25/4 19		Datum: 19		an [Z] z.K.
um: 0643 Uhr		um: Uhr		11. 25/4.
von: 1 242 04		an:		
durch:		durch:		
		Rolle:		

Vermerke:

Chefsache!
Nur durch Offizier

Fernschreiben

+ FRR GHZPH 05/45 25/4 0415.=

-- GKDOS CHEFSACHE NUR DURCH OFFIZIER --.-

Abgangstag	Abgangszeit		

AN REICHSLEITER BORMANN =

	Bestimmungsort

1.) DAS OBERKOMMANDO DER WEHRMACHT IST MIR FUER DIE
FORTFUEHRUNG DER GESAMTOPERATIONEN VERANTWORTLICH..-
2.) ES FUEHRT NACH MEINEN WEISUNGEN, DIE ICH DURCH DEN BEI
MIR BEFINDLICHEN CHEF DES GENSTDH, GEN D INF . KREBS,
UEBERMITTELN LASSE,.-
  A) IM --SUEDRAUM-- MIT HILFE DES FUEHRUNGSSTABES B
     (GENERALLEUTNANT WINTER).-
     H GR SUED UND MITTE,.-
     OB SUEDWEST,.-
     OB SUEDOST,.-
     OB WEST..-
  B) IM --NORDRAUM-- UNMITTELBAR.-
     WB NORWEGEN (GEB AOK 20).-
     WB DAENEMARK.-
     OB NORDWEST.-
     12. ARMEE.-
     HEERESGRUPPE WEICHSEL MIT 9. ARMEE.-
     ARMEE OSTPREUSZEN.-
     HEERESGRUPPE KURLAND..-

Nicht zu übermitteln:

Unterschrift des Aufgebers

Fernsprech-Anschluß des Aufgebers

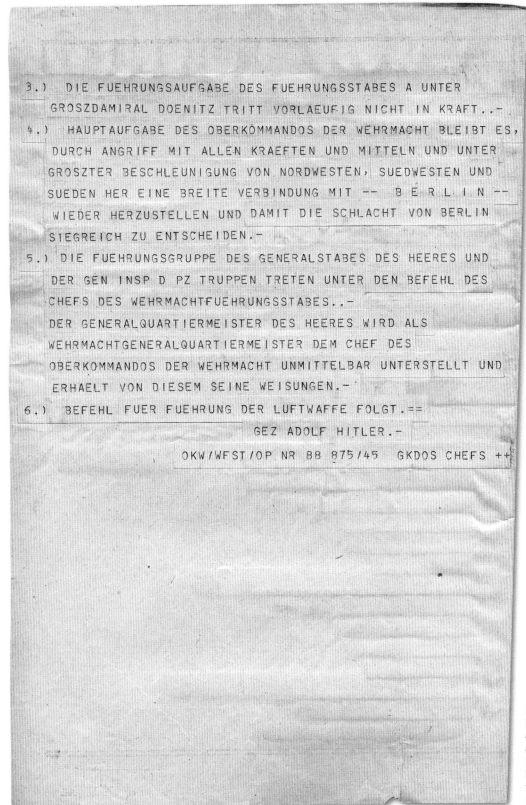

3.) DIE FUEHRUNGSAUFGABE DES FUEHRUNGSSTABES A UNTER
   GROSZDAMIRAL DOENITZ TRITT VORLAEUFIG NICHT IN KRAFT..-
4.) HAUPTAUFGABE DES OBERKOMMANDOS DER WEHRMACHT BLEIBT ES,
   DURCH ANGRIFF MIT ALLEN KRAEFTEN UND MITTELN UND UNTER
   GROSZTER BESCHLEUNIGUNG VON NORDWESTEN, SUEDWESTEN UND
   SUEDEN HER EINE BREITE VERBINDUNG MIT -- B E R L I N --
   WIEDER HERZUSTELLEN UND DAMIT DIE SCHLACHT VON BERLIN
   SIEGREICH ZU ENTSCHEIDEN.-
5.) DIE FUEHRUNGSGRUPPE DES GENERALSTABES DES HEERES UND
   DER GEN INSP D PZ TRUPPEN TRETEN UNTER DEN BEFEHL DES
   CHEFS DES WEHRMACHTFUEHRUNGSSTABES..-
   DER GENERALQUARTIERMEISTER DES HEERES WIRD ALS
   WEHRMACHTGENERALQUARTIERMEISTER DEM CHEF DES
   OBERKOMMANDOS DER WEHRMACHT UNMITTELBAR UNTERSTELLT UND
   ERHAELT VON DIESEM SEINE WEISUNGEN.-
6.) BEFEHL FUER FUEHRUNG DER LUFTWAFFE FOLGT.==
                        GEZ ADOLF HITLER.-
            OKW/WFST/OP NR 88 875/45   GKDOS CHEFS ++

Left and opposite page:
Hitler's last military act. The
original telegram of his orders
concerning Berlin's defense.
Note Bormann's countersign
in the top right corner, and
the red stamp "Chefsache"
reserved for Hitler only.

His obsession was to win the Battle of Berlin, with the political and strategic aim of turning the Allies against the Russians. It is also interesting to note that he did not yet wish to give Dönitz, his future successor, the management of the operations. It shows that he still hoped to win, a hope that rested on his armies still being fit for combat and able to regroup in order to relieve Berlin.

> The main objective for the O.K.W. will be, by means of an all-out attack from the North West, South West and South, to urgently and by all means necessary establish a communications link with Berlin and thus bring about a victory in the Battle for Berlin.

As a result, the armies in Norway,[62] Denmark,[63] Army Group Vistula[64] and Army Group Courland [65] were recalled. In truth this was reorganization that took place on paper only, as most of the elements concerned were unable to obey this order.

Only the 12th Army, already recalled to Army Group Vistula, was in a position to attempt to return to Berlin. This was Wenck's famous army.[66] It was Berlin's last chance. The one on whose shoulders all hopes rested.

After receiving these orders, Wenck ceased combat with the Americans, and answered the call to rescue Berlin. His army, recently formed, suddenly turned east, and in the general confusion, took the Soviets that were surrounding the Reich's capital by surprise. Hitler considered Wenck's breakthrough to be Berlin's last hope.

Wenck's troops set out for Berlin in high spirits but were stopped outside Potsdam by stiff resistance from the Red Army. Unable to reach Berlin, Wenck planned to move towards the Halbe forest to join the remnants of the 9th Army and the Potsdam garrison, who together would open a route to allow the inhabitants of Berlin to escape.

In this moment, one can feel the winds of history brushing past. Between the lines of Bormann's telegrams we can sense the speed and finality of the bunker's residents race towards oblivion. Last telegrams, ultimate traces of life, last steps towards death.

The Last Telegrams

They are presented here in chronological order of transmission.

Telegram *Marinenachrichtendienst*, dated April 23, 1945 at 15:00, marked *Geheim* in red and addressed to Puttkamer[67] in Obersalzberg.

> Urgently telegraph if plane KEIX has landed. Bormann.

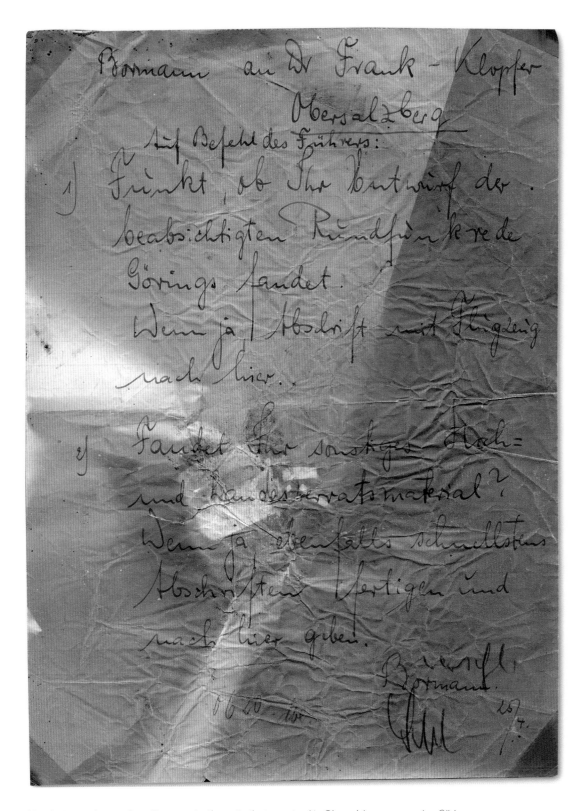

Handwritten telegram from Bormann to the units that remained in Obersalzberg, concerning Göring.

Bormann was worried and wanted to know if Hitler's entourage, who had been allowed to leave the bunker the previous night, had arrived safely in Berchtesgaden. This included Puttkamer and members of various services, as well as SS General Gottlob Berger, Chief of the SS Central Office.

Telegram *Marinenachrichtendienst*, dated April 23, 1945 at 15:12, marked *Geheim* in red and addressed to Puttkamer in Obersalzberg. Half format.

> Telegraph brief overview of the combat situation in the South Germany sector. Things are screwed here. Chief will remain here no matter what. Thus a 180° turn. The mood is clear. Bormann.

By saying "things are screwed," Bormann was probably referring to the various events of the previous days, including the conference of April 22 where Hitler had his most violent outburst. This situation coincided with Göring's telegram the next day. "Chief will remain here no matter what," it was on April 20 that Hitler made the decision to remain in Berlin's combat zone. Then on April 22, after the dramatic staff conference, he announced his irrevocable decision to commit suicide in the bunker, to wait for death in the Reich's capital. "Thus a 180° turn," the idea was still being floated that Hitler could take command of the southern zone and retreat to Bavaria. Puttkamer was one of those primarily concerned with this, as he was in charge of putting everything in place for Hitler's eventual arrival. It is clear that the Hitler's decision to die in Berlin constituted a U-turn. "The mood is clear," these words echo a profoundly dramatic intensity, and say a lot about the cataclysm of the last days in the bunker.

Telegram *Marinenachrichtendienst*, dated April 23, 1945 at 15:30, marked *Geheim* in red and addressed to Müller in Obersalzberg. Half format.

> Let the Führerbau know[68] that only Zander[69] and I are here. Walkenhorst[70] and Hermann are with the Navy staff. We are staying with the Chief in Berlin. Make Ott's inopportune demands stop. We are fighting here. Our future situation depends on Friedrichs[71] and his comrades, who are turning their coats on our enemies. Bormann.

A large number of the people that were in the bunker were dismissed by Hitler. It is the reason why Bormann started the message by listing who was still there.

"We are staying with the Chief in Berlin" testifies to the intense discussions that took place within Hitler's direct circle after he announced the previous day that he

Opposite: Two telegrams sent by Bormann in the last days of April 1945. One of them states: "The Chief will remain here in any case."

Nr. **A**   **Marinenachrichtendienst**   Ltg.-Nr. ....

Aufgen., den 23.4. 1945	Weiter an	Tag	Uhrzeit	Ltg.	durch	
um 1500 Uhr						Uhrzeitgruppe
von .... Ltg.						1158/80
durch Er						**Geheim!**
Verzögerungsverm.						

Fernspruch   Funkspruch   von: **Berlin**
Fernschreiben Posttelegramm

P u t t k a m e r , Oberslazberg

Funkt beeilt, ob Maschine KEIX angekommen.

                    B o r m a n n

Vermerke: erhalten: .... Uhr

Nr. **A**   **Marinenachrichtendienst**   Ltg.-Nr. ....

Aufgen., den 23.4. 1945	Weiter an	Tag	Uhrzeit	Ltg.	durch	
um 1512 Uhr						Uhrzeitgruppe
von .... Ltg.						1141/81
durch Ernst						**Geheim!**
Verzögerungsverm.						

Fernspruch   Funkspruch   von: **Berlin**
Fernschreiben Posttelegramm

P u t t k a m e r , Oberg

Funkt kurzes Kampflagebild über sueddeutschen Raum. Bei uns bumst
es. Chef bleibt auf jeden Fall hier. Daher Wenk 180 Grad. Stimmung
klar.

                    B o r m a n n

Vermerke: erhalten: .... Uhr

Nr.		Marinenachrichtendienst						Ltg.-Nr.

Aufgen., den 23.4. 19 45	Weiter an	Tag	Unrzeit	Ltg.	durch	
um 1530 Uhr						Uhrzeitgruppe
von Ltg.						1135/82
durch Ernst						**Geheim!**
Verzögerungsverm.						

Fernspruch	Funkspruch	von: Berlin
Fernschreiben	Posttelegramm	

M ü l l e r , Obersalzberg

Unterrichtet Führerbau, dass nur noch ich und Zander hier. Walkenhorst und Hermann bei Ob.d.M. Wir bleiben mit Chef in Berlin. Unterbin-
det unzeitgemässe Anfragen von Ott. Hier wird gekämpft. Unser weiteres
Befinden hängt ab von Friedrichs und Genossen, die gegen unseren
Gegner umgeschwenkt.

B o r m a n n

Vermerke: erhalten: .... Uhr

ZMNB Na 690 011
50'CCO x100

On April 23, Bormann ordered that the last members of the Reich's civil administration be thrown into battle.

would commit suicide. The faithful ones made themselves known and it was then that Goebbels decided to bring his family to the bunker. Bormann too decided to remain.

During the night of April 22 to 23, planes were leaving Berlin carrying a great number of Hitler's followers, including Dr. Morell, Julius Schaub, Admiral von Puttkamer and some of the secretaries.

Once more, the "We are fighting here" has an historically interesting dramatic connotation. From April 21, Soviet troops were in the Berlin suburbs and were inexorably advancing towards the center, which they reached four days later. Bormann finishing his telegram with "Our future situation depends on Friedrichs and his companions," perfectly sums up the hopeful expectation of that rescue announced by Hitler. At the same time the "who are turning their coats on our enemies" is proof of the contagious hatred that Hitler displayed towards his generals and armies for betraying him.

The reference to Ott remains unexplained. Is it Eugene Ott? Born in 1889 and died in 1977, he was Germany's ambassador in Japan during World War II. He was also known for having been in touch with spy Richard Sorge. Unless it refers to Wilhelm Höttl, an Austrian SS officer who had an important role in counter intelligence with Kaltenbrunner. From February 1945, Höttl was in touch with the American Office of Strategic Services (O.S.S. the C.I.A.'s predecessor), negotiating a separate peace deal between Austria and the United States. In March, during these negotiations, he met with Allen Dulles, Chief of the Office of Strategic Services, as an intermediary for Kaltenbrunner, but these ended when the U.S.S.R. began occupying Vienna on April 27. He then misled the Allies with the idea of a redoubt in the Alps.

Telegram *Marinenachrichtendienst*, dated April 23, 1945 at 16:00, marked *Geheim* in red and addressed to Giesler[72] in Munich, half format.

The Führer wishes that in your capacity as R.V.K.,[73] you take all the important decisions. Discuss with Klopfer. Immediately send into combat, under appropriate supervision, any superfluous civil service staff. The decision required considering military re-assignments will follow. Bormann.

Note that this item was annotated with a correction in ink, "in" from Bormann's hand. This telegram illustrates well the conduct of total war on which Hitler had decided in these last days. Anyone able to carry a weapon was to be sacrificed "without exception."

Telegram A4 format, dated April 24, 1945 at 00:55, from Dönitz to Reichsleiter Bormann at the Führer's headquarters:

Please designate immediately a Reich's Defense Commissioner for the North Sector to ensure consistent management of all civilian matters. Heil Hitler. Dönitz, Grand Admiral.

The word *Forelle* (Trout) follows, which was his codename. It was on April 20, Hitler decided that, in the event German-controlled territories were cut off by the enemy's advance, they would be divided into a North Sector, under the command of Admiral Karl Dönitz, and a South Sector commanded by Luftwaffe Generalfeldmarschall Albert Kesselring. Dönitz was asking about the creation of a R.V.K. position for the North Sector in the zone under his control. This position had been vacant since April 11, 1945, when its previous holder, North Westphalia Gauleiter Alfred Meyer, committed suicide.

Telegram A4 format, dated April 24, 1945 at 00:55, from Kritzinger[74] to Reichsleiter Bormann at the Führer's headquarters:

Fernschreibstelle _____

WANF 1420.	
Fernschreibname	Laufende Nr.

Angenommen		Befördert:	
Aufgenommen			
Datum: 24.4.45 19__		Datum: 19__	
um: 0055 Uhr:		um: Uhr	
von: OHOKW		an:	
durch: Reutelmar		durch:	
		Rolle:	

Vermerke:

Fernschreiben

++ KR MBGL 520 23.4. (1130)==

AN REICHSLEITER BORMANN FHQU==

Abgangstag	Abgangszeit

Vermerke für Beförderung (vom Aufgeber auszufüllen)	Bestimmungsort

ERBITTE UMGEHEND ERNENNUNG EINES

REICHSVERTEIDIGUNGSKOMMISSARS FUER NORDRAUM ZWECKS

EINHEITLICHER STEUERUNG GESAMTER ZIVILER FRAGEN==

HEIL HITLER,

IHR DOENITZ GROSZADMIRAL(FORELLE)+

Nicht zu übermitteln:

Unterschrift des Aufgebers	Fernsprech-Anschluß des Aufgebers

Grand Admiral Dönitz's telegram to Bormann, dated April 24, and signed with his codename _Forelle_ (trout).

Fernschreibstelle ....

WRYF 1421.
Fernschreibname   Laufende Nr.

Angenommen Aufgenommen		Befördert:	
Datum: 24.4.45 19		Datum: 19	
um: 0055 Uhr:		um: Uhr	
von: O. HOKW		an:	
durch: Heukelmann		durch:	
		Rolle:	

Vermerke:

Fernschreiben

+ KR MBBS 19061 23.4. (1510)==

AN FHQU FUER REICHSLEITER BORMANN==

Abgangstag	Abgangszeit		
Vermerke für Beförderung (vom Aufgeber auszufüllen)			Bestimmungsort

BIN DURCH FUNK UEBER MNA SKL ZU ERREICHEN. WEGEN SUEDFLUGES

HABE ICH MIT WFST. MAJOR BUECHS FUEHLUNG GENOMMEN==

GEZ. STAATSSEKRETAER KRITZINGER+

Nicht zu übermitteln:

Unterschrift des Aufgebers   Fernsprech-Anschluß des Aufgebers

The same day, Bormann was informed of the planes' departure.

> Can be reached by radio via the MNA SKL. Have made contact with Major Buechs regarding flight to South. Staatssekretaer Kritzinger.

This telegram is quite typical of the confusion that dominated the end of the Reich. Indeed, by April 1945, Kritzinger was trying his best to coordinate, from Berlin, the work of the various ministries that were scattered within the decaying Reich. On April 20, he ordered the public servants that were still in Berlin to leave the town and head south, and when it proved impossible to flee by plane, then to flee north, which aggravated Lutz Schwerin von Krosigk who demanded a clear order from Hitler. Kritzinger only managed to obtain from Bormann a recommendation to the ministers and their employees, after which he fled Berlin.

Telegram *Marinenachrichtendienst*, dated April 24, 1945 at 09:10, marked *Geheim* in red and addressed to Reichleiter Bormann from the services in Obersalzberg.

> P.G.[75] Kaltenbrunner[76] expected this morning at 7:00. Dr. Klopfer is already there. Müller.

This document is an interesting communication. Firstly, because it gives an account of the presence of two men in Berchtesgaden, whose positions were closely linked: Klopfer and Kaltenbrunner. It also sheds a new light on Kaltenbrunner's flight. Clearly, he passed through Berchtesgaden before barricading himself in the alpine fortress near Altaussee where he was taken prisoner by U.S. troops on May 12, 1945.

Telegram *Marinenachrichtendienst*, dated April 26, 1945 at 18:20, marked *Geheim* in red and addressed to Backe,[77] Rieke, Klopfer and sent by Bormann.

> Our situation must and will be clarified. The Führer has delayed the decision concerning your request yesterday by a week. This way we will have a better idea of the whole situation. Tell the interested parties. Reichsleiter Bormann.

This text remains quite mysterious. Was this referring to one of the many requests that Hitler should leave Berlin? Unless this was a political or governmental decision. The bunker is still keeping some of its secrets.

On Bormann's desk were also a large number of other documents, which far from the affairs of State that we have just uncovered, concerned the German administration's internal affairs.

The Final Scorch Marks

All the documents, including the most insignificant, were the victims of fire, which proves the importance that the last occupants of the bunker placed on the destruction of all evidence. As proof, many of these pieces are still blackened or damaged by the flames.

There, a folder marked Partei-Kanzlei and a handwritten note in blue ink gave us a half an A4 page, signed in shorthand (untranscribed to this day) and an assortment of news dispatches containing information on: two dispatches (English communications on the start of the Battle of Berlin); Madrid (April 26) on the Spanish situation; Bern (April 26) on the arrest of Jacques Menard, in charge of the Vichy Press; Washington (April 26) on the U.S. civilian population; New York, April 26 (Reuters) on Times Square; April 19, 1945 on Molotov's visit to Washington.

These dispatches are historically very interesting. They were typed by the bunker's operators; whose orders were to transcribe directly from the foreign radios anything

Below and overleaf: Even on April 24 and 26, 1945 the bunker's administration continued to function and receive communications.

Nr. _H_			**Marinenachrichtendienst**					Ltg.-Nr.

Aufgen., den 26.4. 19 45	Weiter an	Tag	Uhrzeit	Ltg.	durch	Uhrzeitgruppe:
um 1820 Uhr						1751/56 FRR
von Ltg.						
durch ml.						**Geheim!**
Verzögerungsverm.						

Fernspruch   Funkspruch   von: **Berlin**

Fernschreiben   Posttelegramm

Backe, Rieke, Klopfer

Unsere Lage muss und wird bereinigt werden. Führer stellte Entschei=
dung über Ihren gestrigen Antrag auf eine Woche zurück. Dann Lage
besser zu übersehen. Unterrichtet von dort aus die Beteiligten.

Reichsleiter Bormann

Vermerk: erhalten:

they could still pick up. In fact, news was getting more and more scarce and no longer reached the bunker. So, to keep abreast of the situation in Berlin, the bunker's occupants had to resort to calling people in the areas of Berlin that still had working phone lines, to get information on the situation in their streets.

Here, a collection of photos, comprising a small photograph showing a couple of original negative films (one of a face, three of dentures) allow us to wonder who these people were. There, another cardboard folder marked *Der Sekretär des Führers* opens a window onto Bormann's daily administrative life. It contains numerous handwritten lines and a blank sheet of headed paper from the Ministry of Foreign Affairs, a memo from the SS Cavalry School in Göttingen, dated January 16, 1945 (partially burnt at the bottom), and six press dispatches (April 21, 1945 Reuters; April 21, 1945 Reuters Stockholm; April 22, 1945 Reuters Madrid; April 22, 1945 Madrid; April 22, 1945 Reuters Madrid; April 22, 1945 Reuters Madrid).

Another folder, orange this time, stamped *Adjudantur der Wehrmacht beim Führer* contained award recommendations. Not just any decoration, but the Third Reich's highest distinction: the Knight's Cross of the Iron Cross. Almost mythical in the history of World War II soldiers, they were still being awarded in the smoldering ruins of Berlin, and were attributed for exceptional merit in combat. And so it was for this recommendation, dated September 19, 1944 for Hans Briegel,[78] 3rd Company, Panzergrenadier Regiment 2, from the Herman Göring Division, signed by a Luftwaffe colonel; and for these two recommendations dated April 18, 1945, concerning Franz Budka,[79] non-commissioned SS officer from the Besslein Regiment; and finally this recommendation for the Knight's Cross of the War Merit Cross with swords, dated October 7, 1944 concerning Colonel Georg von Unold,[80] signed in black ink by Burgdorf,[81] on October 11, 1944.

These documents are doubly emblematic, firstly they concern the highest German decoration, the Knight's Cross of the Iron Cross, and secondly, they represent the very last recipients of this decoration.

Bormann was not only one of the main cogs in the Reich's political administration, he also took his power from his close proximity to Hitler in his role as his private secretary, which is shown in the private archives found in his office.

Below and overleaf: Several documents coming from Bormann's desk. The traces of damp and fire are still obvious. Observe the note coming from an SS cavalry school. Without a doubt, it concerned Hermann Fegelein, the SS Cavalry Commander, who was executed on April 27, in Berlin.

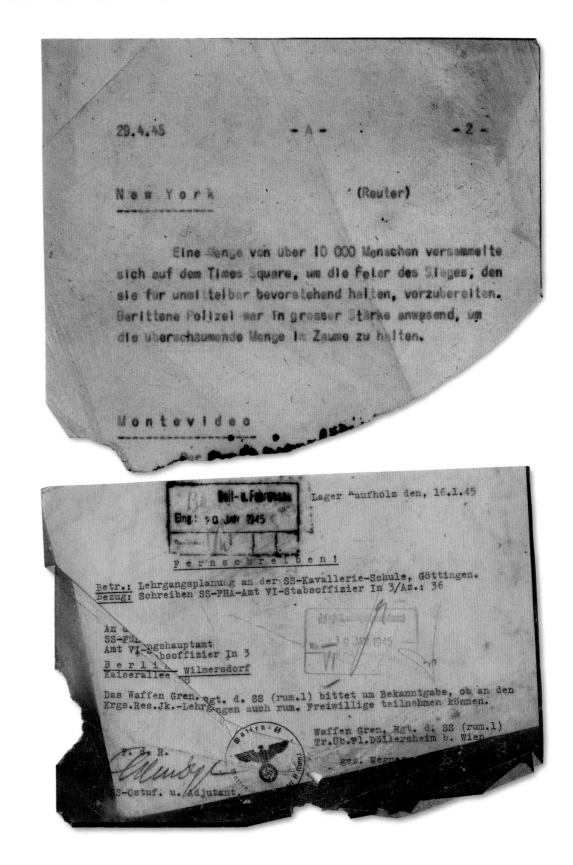

29.4.45   - A -   :   - 2 -

New York   (Reuter)

        Eine Menge von über 10 000 Menschen versammelte
sich auf dem Times Square, um die Feier des Sieges, den
sie für unmittelbar bevorstehend halten, vorzubereiten.
Berittene Polizei war in grosser Stärke anwesend, um
die überschäumende Menge in Zaume zu halten.

Montevideo

Lager Saufholz den, 16.1.45

Eing.: 20 JAN 1945

F e r n s c h r e i b e n !

Betr.: Lehrgangsplanung an der SS-Kavallerie-Schule, Göttingen.
Bezug: Schreiben SS-FHA-Amt VI-Stabsoffizier In 3/Az.: 36

An
SS-Führungshauptamt
Amt VI-Stabsoffizier In 3
B e r l i n - Wilmersdorf
Kaiserallee

Das Waffen Gren. Rgt. d. SS (rum.1) bittet um Bekanntgabe, ob an den
Krgs.Res.Jk.-Lehrgängen auch rum. Freiwillige teilnehmen können.

                           Waffen Gren. Rgt. d. SS (rum.1)
                           Tr.Üb.Pl.Döllersheim b. Wien

F. d. R.   gez. Wegner

SS-Ostuf. u. Adjutant.

Left: Knight's Cross of the Iron Cross (left) and the War Merit Cross. (*Hermann Historica*)

Below: A recommendation for the award of the Knight's Cross of the Iron Cross found on Bormann's desk.

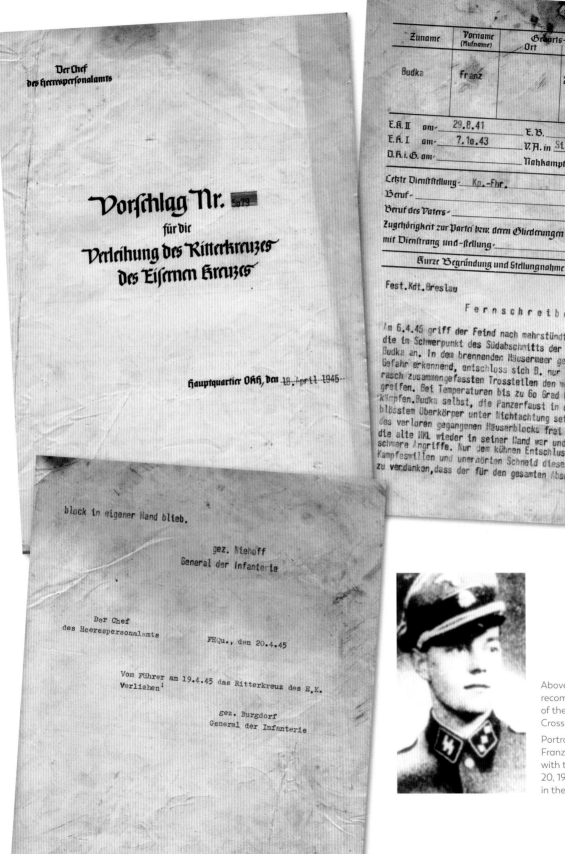

Der Chef
des Heerespersonalamts

Vorschlag Nr. 5079
für die
Verleihung des Ritterkreuzes
des Eisernen Kreuzes

Hauptquartier OKH, den 18. April 1945

Zuname	Vorname (Rufname)	Geburts- Ort	Tag	Dienstgrad	Truppenteil
Budka	Franz		2o.8.2o	SS-U Stuf.	SS-Rgt. Besslein

E.K.II am 29.8.41			E.B.	am	
E.K.I am 7.1o.43			V.A. in Silber	am 4.4.44	
D.K.i.G. am			Nahkampfsp. Stufe am		

Letzte Dienststellung Kp.-Fhr.

Beruf seit

Beruf des Vaters

Zugehörigkeit zur Partei bzw. deren Gliederungen

mit Dienstrang und -stellung

Kurze Begründung und Stellungnahme der Zwischen-Vorgesetzten:

Fest.Kdt. Breslau   den 17.4.1945

F e r n s c h r e i b e n !

Am 6.4.45 griff der Feind nach mehrstündiger Trommelfeuervorbereitung die im Schwerpunkt des Südabschnitts der Festung eingesetzte Komp. Budka an. In dem brennenden Häusermeer gelang ihm ein Einbruch. Die Gefahr erkennend, entschloss sich B. nur mit seinem Kp.-Trupp und rasch zusammengefassten Trossteilen den weit überlegenen Gegner anzu-greifen. Bei Temperaturen bis zu 6o Grad kam es zu erbitterten Nah-kämpfen. Budka selbst, die Panzerfaust in der Hand, kämpfte mit ent-blösstem Oberkörper unter Nichtachtung seiner Person Keller um Keller des verloren gegangenen Häuserblocks frei und ruhte nicht eher, bis die alte HKL wieder in seiner Hand war und hielt diese gegen 8 weitere schwere Angriffe. Nur dem kühnen Entschluss, sowie dem verbissenen Kampfeswillen und unerhörten Schneid dieses vorbildlichen Offz. ist es zu verdanken, dass der für den gesamten Abschnitt entscheidende Häuser-

block in eigener Hand blieb.

gez. Niehoff
General der Infanterie

Der Chef
des Heerespersonalamts   FHQu., den 20.4.45

Vom Führer am 19.4.45 das Ritterkreuz des E.K.
Verliehen!

gez. Burgdorf
General der Infanterie

Above and left: The recommendation for the award of the Knight's Cross of the Iron Cross to Franz Budka.

Portrait: Untersturmführer Franz Budka was decorated with the Ritterkreuz on April 20, 1945, while he was fighting in the fortress of Breslau.

**Der Chef
des Heerespersonalamts**

Vorschlag Nr. ▨▨▨

für die

Verleihung des Ritterkreuzes

des

Kriegsverdienstkreuzes

mit Schwertern

Hauptquartier OKH, den ......

Left, below and overleaf: Recommendation for the award of the Knight's Cross of the War Merit Cross to Georg von Unold.

Zuname	Vorname (Rufname)	Geburts-Ort	Tag	Dienstgrad	Truppenteil
von Unold	Georg	Tettau Krs. Teuschnitz	23.12. 1905	Oberst i.G. O.Qu.	Obkdo.d. H.Gr. Mitte

EK. 2. Klasse am:	31.5.1940	KVK. 2. Klasse am:	
EK. 1. Klasse am:	30.7.1940	KVK. 1. Klasse am:	
DK. in Gold am:	9.10.1942	DK. in Silber am:	
Ostmedaille	1.8.1942		

Letzte Dienststellung: O.Qu. ; seit: 1. Juni 1942
Beruf: aktiv
Beruf des Vaters: Forstmeister (gestorben)
Heimatanschrift: Neuhaus am Schliersee Obb.

Kurze Begründung und Stellungnahme der Zwischenvorgesetzten:

Oberkommando der Heeresgruppe Mitte , den 29.Aug.1944

Oberst i.G.von Unold wurde nach hervorragender Bewährung als Ia der 10.Pz.Gren.Div. am 1.6.42 Oberquartiermeister der Außenstelle OKH/Gen.Qu. Befehlsstelle Mitte und am 10.9.1942 bei Aufstellung einer Oberquartiermeister-Abteilung im Oberkommando der H.Gr. Oberquartiermeister der H. Gr. Mitte und wurde damit für die Gesamtversorgung dieser lange Zeit hindurch stärksten deutschen Heeresgruppe verantwortlich. Rund 44.000 Mann Versorgungstruppen in 600 Versorgungseinheiten und -Einrichtungen sind ihm einsatzmäßig unterstellt.
Dank überragender Begabung und eingehender Kenntnis der Versorgungsführung und der letzten Einzelheiten ihrer prakti-

schen Arbeit sowie unermüdlicher schöpferischer Schaffens-
freude hat er diese Aufgabe in über 2 Jahren schwerster
Kampfe glänzend gelöst und die Oberbefehlshaber der H.Gr.
weitblickend und richtig beraten.
Stets persönlich an den für die Kampfversorgung gerade
wichtigsten Brennpunkten anwesend und eingreifend, war
Oberst i.G. von Unold die Seele der Heeresversorgung an der
mittleren Ostfront. Neben der klaren generalstabsmäßigen
Vorbereitung der Angriffsoperationen und der raschen Schwer-
punktbildung im Verlaufe der oft wechselvollen Abwehrkämp-
fe sind die bei allen Schwierigkeiten reibungslos durchge-
führten Raumungsmaßnahmen 1943 sein besonderes Verdienst;so
die "Büffel-Bewegung" aus dem Raum Rshew-Wjasma, die Räu-
mung des Orel-Bogens, wo beim Durchstoß des Feindes auf
Karatschew und Ausfall der Bahn der O.Qu. persönlich von
Brjansk aus in 12 Stunden den gesamten Großtransportraum
der Heeresgruppe mit rund 8.000 to zusammenfaßte und damit
der 9. und der 2.Panzer Armee die Fortsetzung des Kampfes
ermöglichte, und die großräumige Absetzbewegung der H.Gr.
Mitte auf die Dnjepr-Linie.
Die Raschheit und einfallsreiche Wendigkeit der Versorgungsführung durch Oberst i.G. von Unold haben schließlich ent-
scheidenden Anteil an der Wiederherstellung der Lage im
mittleren Abschnitt der Ostfront in diesem Sommer. Der vor-
ausschauende Aufbau einer Versorgungs-Basis für die neu
herangeführten Verbande, Auffangen und Neugliederung der
Versorgungstruppen und -einrichtungen und die Steuerung der
Raumung sind sein Werk. Bezeichnend für die Leistungen von
Oberst i.G. von Unold ist seine Vielseitigkeit, die sich
bis in die letzte Einheit auswirkt und sich kei
die Steuerung und Verteilung der militärischen
güter beschränkt.
Besonders intensiv war seine Einflußnahme in a
wirtschaftlichen Fragen. Den Betrieben des Hee
Wirtschaftsführers wurde durch ein weitblicken
Programm" die Richtung gewiesen und damit ein
liche Leistung für die Truppe erreicht.
Von unmittelbarem Einfluß auf die Kampffuhrur
seine dauernde Einflußnahme auf die Panzer-In
wo ihm neben der Erkenntnis der Wichtigkeit
hohen fachtechnischen Kenntnisse zugute kame
wesentlich sein Verdienst, daß der H.Gr.Mitt

Martin Bormann's Archives

The main item is an imposing folder of correspondence with Arthur Kannenberg, a significant correspondence which illustrates the scope of business that Bormann dealt with in the name of his Führer. Nothing seems trivial.

Through these pages we find: the draft of a letter to Hitler, dating from 1943 and signed by Kannenberg with his handwritten corrections; three letters on India paper from Kannenberg (one to Hitler, two to Bormann); two letters signed by Bormann to Kannenberg dating from 1943; a three-page copy of a letter on India

Zeit schwerster Kampfe ein ungewöhnlich hoher Prozentsatz
einsatzfähiger Panzer zur Verfügung stand.
Oberst i.G. von Unold ist als überragender Oberquartiermeiste
auf Grund seiner Persönlichkeit und seiner ungewöhnlichen
Leistungen der beantragten hohen Auszeichnung im besonderen
Maße würdig.

gez. K r e b s
Generalleutnant
und Chef des Gen.Stabes d.H.Gr.Mitte
Oberkommando der H.Gr. Mitte   , den 30.8.1944
Ich befürworte den Vorschlag.

Der Oberbefehlshaber
m.d.F.b.
gez. Reinhardt
Generaloberst

Der Chef
des Heerespersonalamts

Führerhauptquartier, den 11.10.44

Befürwortet!

F.W.

Generalleutnant

paper; two letters from Kannenberg to Bormann (only one of them signed), a greeting card from the Führer's *Adjundantur* (Christmas 1942) signed by Burgdorf, von Puttkamer and Nicolaus von Below;[82] a correspondence between Kurt Böhning and Kannenberg; a sheet of India paper replicating a letter of good wishes for 1942 addressed to Eva Braun; a series of copies of letters from Kannenberg addressed to various people dating from 1942; a letter signed by the Korpsführer of the NSKK,[83] correspondence between Bruno Heroux[84] to Kannenberg, with copies of Kannenberg's answers.

Arthur Kannenberg (1896–1963) was Hitler's steward. He studied gastronomy with his father, Oskar Kannenberg, who owned a hotel and several restaurants in Berlin. His restaurants were very popular with the Nazis before they came to power, and with Hitler in particular. Soon Arthur Kannenberg was asked to take care of the Brown House in Munich. Once Hitler was in power, Kannenberg was made steward of the Reich chancellery in Berlin. His job also entailed taking care of the Führer's headquarters and the Berghof. In the bunker, he occupied a place called the Kannenberg Alley, where the provisions were kept.

A rare color photograph of Martin Bormann in his honorary SS Gruppenführer uniform.

His duties placed him under Bormann, who was among other things the Berghof's supervisor. It is therefore normal that their correspondence should be mixed, which gives us another insight into Hitler's entourage.

Even more personal was a very damaged orange cardboard folder, which reveals an A4 color drawing, signed Eicke[85] and dated 1945. Eicke was one of Martin Bormann's daughters. The picture was drawn on the back of his paper at Obersalzberg, where his family had taken refuge. A few grams of paper bringing a little light and love in this dreary and morbid atmosphere.

Between two decorations recovered at random during their visit in the corridors of the bunker, a first class Iron Cross and a Mother's Cross of Honor,[86] and also a number of books, the bunker's visitors discovered an album blackened by soot. It was a striking piece, a collection of original ink drawings having belonged to Otto Günsche,[87] and representing the town of Rastenburg, and more particularly the Wolfsschanze Complex, Hitler's main H.Q. in the east. This collection was given to him as a birthday

present on September 24, 1944. It contains 8 pages of satirical pictures illustrating daily life in Hitler's H.Q. The first page shows the letters E.R., which were the artist's initials.

From one bunker to another... an album that concludes a lengthy journey through time.

A drawing from one of Bormann's daughters to her father, done on the back of his Obersalzberg-headed paper.

Berlin ~~Mai 1943~~

Herrn

Reichsleiter M. Bormann

Führerhauptquartier

Sehr geehrter Herr Reichsleiter Bormann !

Unsere grosse Freude über die vom Führer verfügte Erhöhung
unseres Gehaltes wollen wir Ihnen hiermit zum Ausdruck bringen.
Nehmen wir doch an, dass Sie - Herr Reichsleiter - sicherlich
hierzu die Veranlassung gegeben haben.
Wir bedanken uns sehr herzlich dafür und freuen uns besonders
darüber, dass das uns so lange schon vom Führer zugedachte
Monatsgehalt in der Höhe ausgezahlt wird, wie es der Führer von
Anfang an bestimmt hatte. Lediglich der Einspruch des Herrn
R. Hess und W.Brückner hiergegen vereitelte die Auszahlung der
uns vom Führer beim Engagement im Februar 1933 zugebilligten
Summe in Höhe von RM 1.ooo,-- für meine Leistungen; die Leistung
meiner Frau sollte extra entschädigt werden.

Wir unterstellten uns diesem Wunsche der Herren seinerzeit ohne
Protest, um hiermit zu dokumentieren, dass uns nicht so viel an
dem Geld lag, als an der Ehre, die hohe Aufgabe, unserem Führer
zu dienen, ergebenst auszuführen.

Die uns ausgezahlte Summe betrug bis zum Jahre 1937 RM 600,--
netto pro Monat für uns beide. Diese Summe wurde dann plötzlich
auf RM 1.2oo,-- erhöht gelegentlich eines Aufenthaltes in Nürn-
berg 1937 im Hotel Deutscher Hof, nachdem der Führer in Erfahrung
gebracht hatte, dass der Hoteldirektor R
Gehalt erhielt. Herr Hauptmann Wiedemann
den Erhöhungsauftrag unseres Einkommens,

Ich teilte wiederum diese Summe in zwei
~~leistungen meiner Frau den Leistungen u~~
~~arbeiters gleichstellte.~~

Documents coming from Arthur Kannenberg's
folder.

Von diesen Vorgängen ~~dachten~~ wir Ihnen nun einmal Kenntnis
geben ~~zu müssen~~, umsomehr sich hierzu eine passende Gelegen-
heit ~~ergibt~~.
Wir ~~freuten~~ uns sehr über diese Anerkennungsgebühr unserer
Leistungen, mit denen wir den Führer seit 1o Jahren immer
treu und ergeben umsorgt haben.

Wir grüssen Sie, Herr Reichsleiter,

mit

Sieg Heil !
Ihre

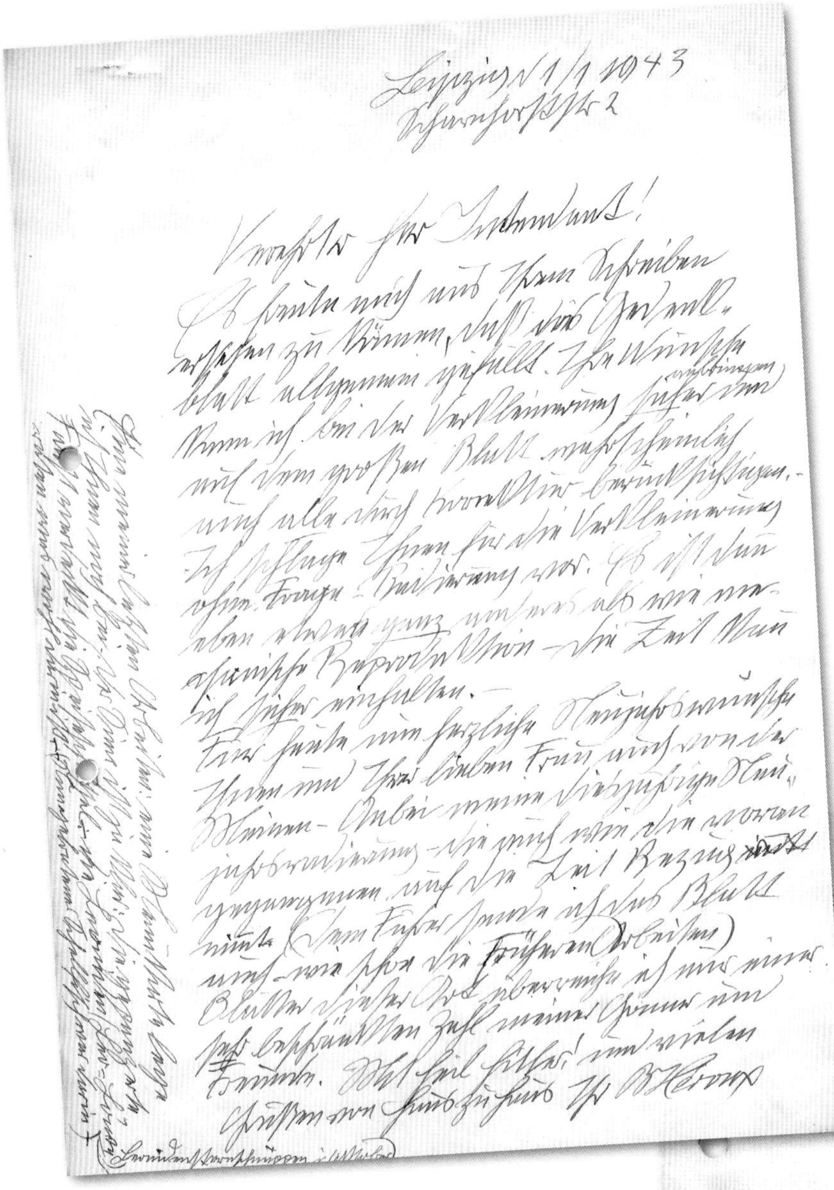
Leipzig 1/1 1943

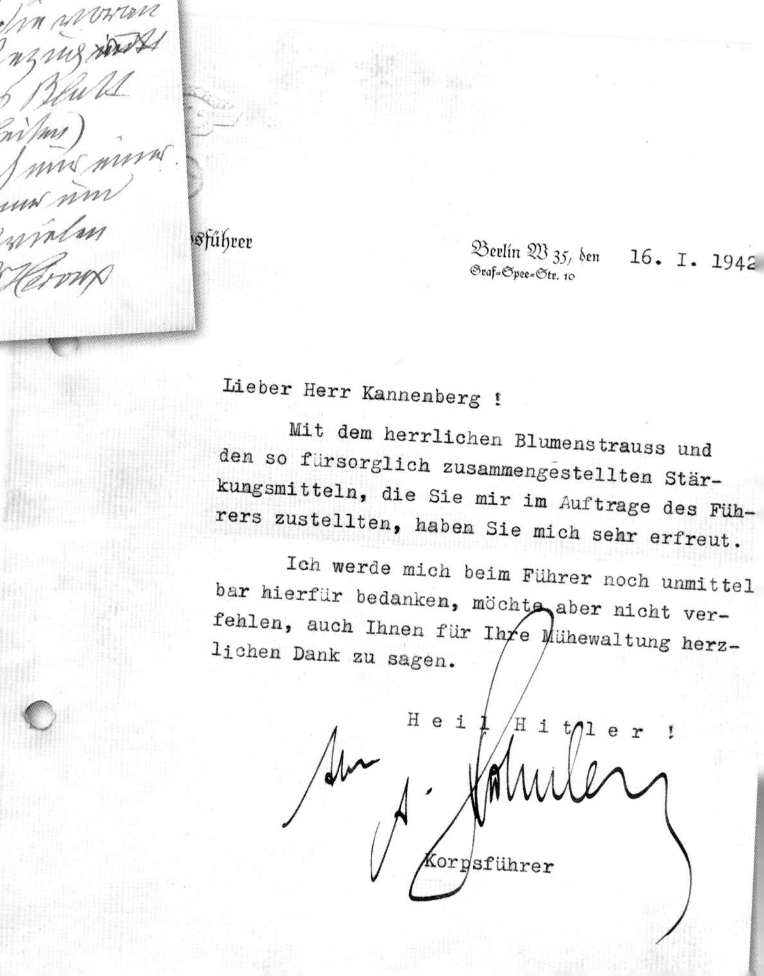

…sführer

Berlin W 35, den 16. I. 1942
Graf-Spee-Str. 10

Lieber Herr Kannenberg !

Mit dem herrlichen Blumenstrauss und den so fürsorglich zusammengestellten Stärkungsmitteln, die Sie mir im Auftrage des Führers zustellten, haben Sie mich sehr erfreut.

Ich werde mich beim Führer noch unmittelbar hierfür bedanken, möchte aber nicht verfehlen, auch Ihnen für Ihre Mühewaltung herzlichen Dank zu sagen.

Heil Hitler !

Korpsführer

More documents from Arthur Kannenberg's folder.

Otto Günsche, in the foreground, was Hitler's personal aide-de-camp. He was among the last of the faithful, and was the one who burned Hitler and Eva Braun's bodies. In the background is Hermann Junge who married Traudl Humps.

RASTENBURG. 1944

Right: Cover page of the booklet given to Otto Günsche for his birthday on September 24, 1944.

Overleaf: Drawings from the same booklet, depicting life in Hitler's H.Q. in Rastenburg.

SEHENSWÜRDIGKEITEN IN RASTENBURG.

RATHAUS

SCHLOSS.

AUTOHOF

HINDENBURGSTRASSE 5

SO   ODER   SO

IST   DAS   LEBEN - -

MAN WÜRDE OFTMALS
    VIEL DRUM GEBEN
WÄRS SO: WIE LINKS
            ZU SEHEN!
DOCH IST ES AUCH NICHT
            SCHLECHT
IST'S SO: „WIE RECHTS" - -

DRUM, WIE'S AUCH WIRD
    IM LEBEN,
WAS MAN SICH WÜNSCHT,
        ODER WILL GEBEN -
AM ENDE IST ES IMMER
            GLEICH:
„S'KOMMT ALLES SCHON
    ZU SEINER ZEIT"!

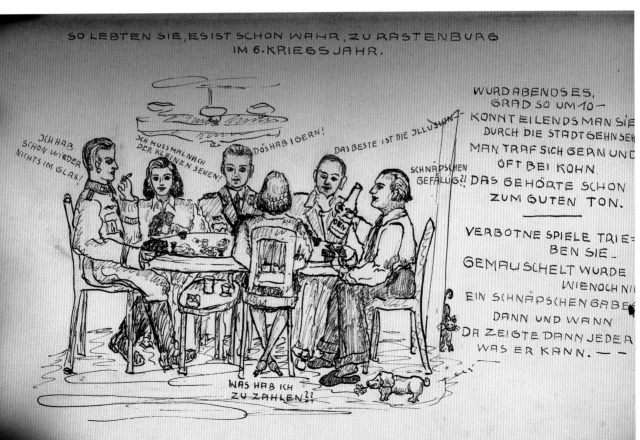

ES TANZT EIN JEDER WIE ER KANN
MANCHER HÄLT ABSTAND UND MANCHER
GEHT RAN—

OFT GAB ES AUCH EIN SOLOTÄNZCHEN
UND WAR ES SCHÖN, WÜNSCHT MAN SICH
EIN „SCHWÄNZCHEN"

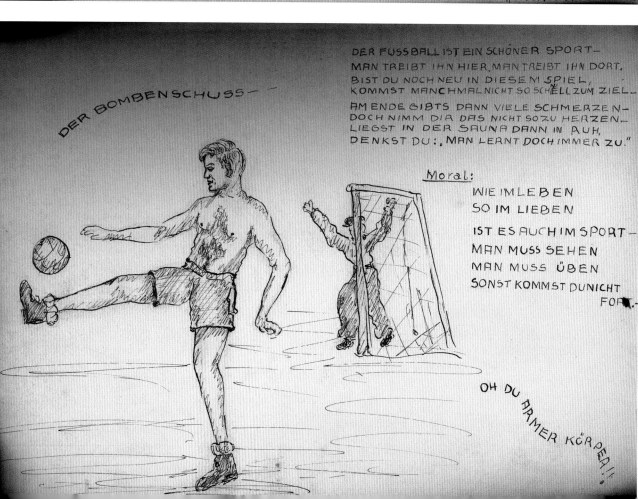

DER BOMBENSCHUSS—

DER FUSSBALL IST EIN SCHÖNER SPORT—
MAN TREIBT IHN HIER, MAN TREIBT IHN DORT.
BIST DU NOCH NEU IN DIESEM SPIEL,
KOMMST MANCHMAL NICHT SO SCHNELL ZUM ZIEL—
AM ENDE GIBTS DANN VIELE SCHMERZEN—
DOCH NIMM DIR DAS NICHT SO ZU HERZEN—
LIEGST IN DER SAUNA DANN IN AUH,
DENKST DU:, MAN LERNT DOCH IMMER ZU."

Moral:

WIE IM LEBEN
SO IM LIEBEN

IST ES AUCH IM SPORT—
MAN MUSS SEHEN
MAN MUSS ÜBEN
SONST KOMMST DU NICHT
FORT.—

OH DU ARMER KÖRPER !!

Several objects and documents found near Bormann's desk. Of note, an Iron Cross 1st Class, and more surprising, a Mother's Cross of Honor. The paper disks were used to seal letters from the Adjutantur der Wehrmacht beim Fuhrer (General Wilhelm Burgdorf).

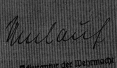

Adjutantur der Wehrmacht
beim Führer

Appendices: Portraits

MARTIN BORMANN OR "HITLER'S BULL"

Martin Bormann. (*Hermann Historica*)

Martin Bormann was born in 1900, his father, Theodor, a postal worker and former Sergeant Major in the Prussian army, was a deeply pious Protestant. In fact, his son was named after Martin Luther, the founder of the Protestant reform. Perhaps it is here that one can find the first spark of hate that Martin Bormann would feel all his life for religions.

Bormann quickly dropped his studies to work on a farm in Mecklenburg. War soon found him though, and he was mobilized in an artillery regiment. His presence at the front seems to have been as short as it was dull. The end of the war and the new Weimar Republic pushed him into entering the Freikorps,[88] more precisely the Rossbach[89] Freikorps.

Gerhard Rossbach not benefiting from the best reputation, it is not surprising that Martin Bormann's name found itself associated with various murders during his time there. In March 1924, he was sentenced to a year in prison as the accomplice of Rudolf Hess (who was to become Auschwitz's commander) for the brutal murder of Walther Kadow (former primary school teacher), who had likely betrayed Leo Schlageter[90] during the French occupation of the Ruhr.

He joined the N.S.D.A.P. after leaving prison and became regional press officer in Thuringia and in 1928, was promoted to Director. From 1928 to 1930, he was Supreme Command Attaché for the SA, and in October 1933, he became Reichleiter of the N.S.D.A.P. A month later, he was an elected member of the Reichstag.

His rapid ascension was due to his bureaucratic abilities. Indeed, he seemed made for this type of work. Diligent, adaptable, efficient, brutal, with no scruples or mercy, he embodied the perfect Nazi official. To complete the picture, he bore uncommonly deep grudges and was very efficient in getting his potential opponents out of the way.

His discreet rise to the top of the Nuremberg podium was helped by Hitler's closest ally: Rudolf Hess. The latter occupied a privileged position as Hitler's deputy during the first years of the Nazi movement. So much so, that in 1933 Hitler publicly called him his successor. Referred to as the "Party's conscience," he had great influence thanks to his position and close relationship with Hitler.

From July 1933 until 1941, Bormann was Hess' Chief of Staff, personal secretary and right-hand man. As such, he not only had access to immense power, but above all he benefited from an intimacy with Adolf Hitler, whether in his public or private affairs. He was at the core of the Nazi Party.

A model secretary, he patiently and diligently spun his web to become the indispensable right-hand man, the man in the shadows who had all the files at his disposal. His rise to power was facilitated by three factors. Firstly, Hitler was not a clerical man, he made plans, gave directions, but left his subordinates to take care of the actual realization. From his youth as a Viennese artist, he retained this slightly bohemian side, and dwelled more happily in ideas and theories than in administration. This is what rapidly made Martin Bormann indispensable to Hitler and let him acquire complete control over the system's bureaucracy and gain Hitler's personal trust. Baldur von Schirach's memoir is a good illustration of this, he quotes Hitler saying to him:

> Put this in your head, I need Bormann to win this war. Yes, he is brutal and without scruples. He is a bull. But everyone should know that if they disapprove of Bormann, they disapprove of me, and I will get anyone who opposes that man, shot.[91] Secondly, his ascension was facilitated by the very character of the man he depended on: Rudolf Hess. Whilst Hess had great influence, his sole objective was to serve Hitler, and he happily ignored is own ambitions. As time went on, his position became more withdrawn, at a distance from the intrigues of the regime's highest circle. This attitude isolated him though, and lessened his political influence. He limited himself to giving a few speeches every year, like at Christmas; to receiving delegations of the Alliance of German Organizations Abroad, or to taking coffee with mothers of large families and taking up charitable tasks, like the patronage of some lesser conventions. He kept the privilege of announcing Hitler's arrival during solemn ceremonies.

This marginalization of his political role increased during the first years of World War II, which focused on strategists rather than politicians. He was, however, named a member of the Reich Defense Council in 1939, and assisted Hitler on June 21, 1940 in the preparations for the French armistice of 1940 at Rethondes. His flight to England in 1941 finally wiped him from the political chessboard. The more Rudolf Hess' influence diminished, the more Bormann's grew. He was the man to replace him and keep the Party's administration running, which should have been Hess' responsibility.

Finally, one of his duties would seal this new bond with Hitler, his position as Administrator for all the buildings and grounds of the Obersalzberg in Berchtesgaden, and Hitler's chalet, the Berghof in particular. The Führer was passionate about his Alpine retreat and its beautiful vista. He felt at home there and spent half his time there between 1933 and 1945.

As it became the unofficial second capital of the Reich, Bormann's function as organizer of the place played a capital importance in his relationship with Hitler, and in the latter's trust in him. Bormann put all his considerable zeal into it. Detested by the locals as much as by the vast administration he directed on the spot, he was nicknamed the "Lord of Obersalzberg." He enriched himself in all kinds of ways, including in Berchtesgaden where he acquired for himself two thirds of the expropriated lands and the nicest houses. But he also got rich by developing and administrating the endowments of funds from German industry, and the vast donations from many businessmen to Hitler.

He married Gerta Buch (1909–1946), a devoted Nazi and daughter of the Party's Supreme Court Judge, Walter Buch, with whom he had ten children, among them Martin Bormann Jr (1930–2013). They were a close couple, albeit an unconventional one: his wife thriving on his feminine conquests, and hopeful in January 1944, that one of them, actress Manja Behrens, would give him another child. Together with his wife, he would during 1944, write a proposition of law authorizing bigamy in the Reich.

Avowedly anti-Christian and anti-clerical, he often emphasized the incompatibility between Nazism and Christianity, and favored the persecution of Catholic and Protestant churches. He wrote:

> National-Socialist concepts are incompatible with Christianity. The work of Christian churches was based on human ignorance, whilst National-Socialism is based on science.

As is often the case with second-rate characters who have acquired their power thanks to base intrigues, their final triumphs are favored by dramatic events that project them to the front of the stage. This is exactly what happened to Martin Bormann in the last concrete-filled days of April 1945, where confined with his master, he finally became the sole access to the Führer.

This is how he became puppet master of the last marionettes in a wrecked landscape. After Hitler's suicide, some of the Führerbunker's occupants decided to flee the Soviet advance. On the evening of May 1:

> Bormann and Mohnke tried to organize the staff to be evacuated into several groups. These groups departed around 23:00, two hours later than planned. [...] For a while, Bormann, Stumpfegger, Schwägermann and Axmann remained together. They followed the railway line as far as the Lehrterstrasse Station. They then split up. Bormann and Stumpfegger went northeast towards Stettin Station. Axmann went in the opposite direction, but met with a Soviet patrol, and had to retrace his steps, following Bormann. A little later, he found two corpses, he identified them as Bormann and Stumpfegger, but did not have time to ascertain how they had been killed.[92] In the chaos

of Berlin's fall, the corpses were not located, creating rumors of a possible escape. Due to the uncertainty surrounding his disappearance, Bormann was sentenced to death *in absentia* during the Nuremberg trials for war crimes and crimes against humanity.

It was the start of a long list of fantasies and historical hallucinations, where Bormann was said to have been seen walking around various South American countries that he had reached by submarine, the last ghost ship of the regime. It wasn't until December 7, 1972, that two corpses re-opened the debate. They were discovered during building works near Lehrter Station, and matched Artur Axmann's testimony. These skeletons were quickly identified as those of Bormann and Stumpfegger thanks to their teeth. Prosthetist Fritz Echtmann recognized the three-part bridge that he had made himself for Bormann in 1942.

Glass found between his teeth indicated that he had committed suicide with a cyanide pill. On April 4, 1973, the Frankfurt prosecutor officially recognized Bormann's death on the basis of Reidar Sognnaes' dental expertise. In 1998 the findings were confirmed by a D.N.A. test led by Dr. W. Eisenmenger, from the Munich Legal Medical Institute

ADOLF HITLER'S PERSONAL SECURITY

At the very heart of a state that was one of the most heavily policed of its time, the organization of its leader's security is a particularly interesting subject. Originally, Hitler's close security was entrusted to a small group, recruited among his war comrades, like Sergeant Max Amann.[93] As his importance on the political chessboard increased, his security had to be increased too. Hitler having only a limited trust in the Sturmabteilungen (SA), he decided to create a small unit dedicated only to his protection. This was how in 1923, the Stosstrupp-Hitler was founded.

In 1925, the Schutzstaffel, or SS, was created, a small formation of a hundred men or so in charge of Hitler's protection who would, although initially subordinate to the SA, play a major role in the history of the Third Reich.

The scale that the SS reached had consequences for Hitler's small protection unit; it needed to evolve further. And so was born, in February 1932, the SS Begleitkommando des Führers, specifically created to

protect him during his trips and in charge of his security. This unit comprised eight persons charged with his protection night and day. Whatever change of names they would see, these eight men would stay by Hitler's side until his cremation in the Berlin chancellery.

On April 30, 1933, beneath the balconies of the Reichstag, SA troops marched in the torchlight. Hitler had just been named Reich Chancellor by von Hindenburg. Protection missions multiplied, and the number of men was too small.

Power would change that. On March 15, 1933, two and a half months after his ascension to the title of Chancellor, the Führerschutzkommando was created, which on August 1, 1935 finally became the Reichssicherheitsdienst, or R.S.D. and whose kommandeur until the end of the war was Johann Rattenhuber.

The Führerschutzkommando was originally composed of men from the Bavaria Criminal Police, and specifically

Gruppenführer Johann Rattenhuber, Reichssicherheitsdienst (R.S.D.) commander.

In order to wear the black and silver uniform, candidates had to supply an imposing file attesting to their Aryan status. The R.S.D. missions were now on a much wider scale than those of the original Begleitkommando des Führers.

As well as Hitler's personal protection at home and away, the R.S.D. was in charge of leading any investigation pertaining to potential assassination plans on his person, but also to monitor the buildings of the towns he visited[95] and the building he lived in.

To fulfil their missions, the R.S.D. could commandeer the assistance of all units and local services. Their background in criminal police afforded them great powers of investigation and arrest. They answered directly to Hitler, so Rattenhuber did not have to go through Himmler for his orders.

In time, the R.S.D. missions would increase drastically. They would become the Führer's guardian angels, taking care of everything in the minutest detail: his private staff, civil or military,[96] checking his mail and parcels for potential threats, his switchboard, his movies, his food, his trips, all the way to the flowers that were placed on his table. A detailed study of this unit would no doubt shed an interesting light on Hitler's private life. He did not try to hide his affection for his precious entourage. He gave them complete leeway, and no one was allowed to criticize them. He was aware of their utter devotion,[97] and it was the reason why he entrusted to them only the task of burning his body after his suicide on April 30, 1945.

Their usual area of activity before the war, was mostly the new chancellery in Berlin, Munich where Hitler owned a private apartment on Printzregenten Platz, and Berchtesgaden where they lodged in the former Zum Türken hotel, located above the Berghof. The most delicate surveillance missions took place during the war, and more particularly during his travels to the front. This was why the O.K.W. granted them the status of Reichssicherheitsdienst Gruppe Geheime Feldpolizei (Secret Military Police), allowing them to receive unconditional and immediate assistance from all regular units at the front, like the Feldgendarmerie, but also to investigate and enter all zones and military buildings, and to wear any army uniform if required.

The R.S.D. also took care of protection for other public figures from the regime. In 1944, the R.S.D. detachments

recruited in Munich. However, their authority was territorial only, not national, which was a serious drawback in their missions, as Hitler travelled the whole of Germany. The issue was solved with the creation of the R.S.D., as its name indicated it became a Reich security service, which gave it nation-wide authority. According to its establishment documents, its members were chosen from among true National Socialists, who doubled as excellent criminal police officers of an "exceptional reliability," and with an "extreme conscientiousness in doing their duty." Furthermore, they had to be in excellent physical condition and of good character.

On November 9, 1935 they swore an oath in front of Hitler and Himmler, outside the Third Reich's symbolic building, the Munich Feldherrnhalle.[94] Members of the R.S.D. were not yet all SS, but this would change on May 1, 1937, as Himmler wished in this way to strengthen the web he was spinning around the regime.

were as follows: 1. Adolf Hitler & Obersalzberg, 2. Hermann Göring, 3. Joachim von Ribbentrop, 4. Heinrich Himmler, 5. Joseph Goebbels, 6. Wilhelm Frick, 7. Hans Frank (Prague), 8. Munich, 9. Berchtesgaden, 10. Artur Seyss-Inquart (The Hague), 11. Josef Terboven (Oslo), 12. Karl Dönitz, 13. Werner Best (Copenhagen), 14. Ernst Kaltenbrunner. As well as: Robert Ley, Erich Koch and Sicherheits-Kontrolldienst Reichskanzlei.

It is interesting to note that some of the telegrams taken by Capitaine Leroy in the bunker, were addressed to R.S.D. 1, which was in charge of protecting Hitler and the Obersalzberg.

Apart from this bodyguard unit, Hitler also had an honor and escort unit that was in keeping with his function. That was the Leibstandarte SS Adolf Hitler or L.S.S.A.H., officially created on March 17, 1933 by SS officer "Sepp" Dietrich, Hitler's personal bodyguard, under the name SS-Stabswache Berlin. Note that the insignia of the L.S.S.A.H. was a master key, "Dietrich" in German.

The headquarters of the L.S.S.A.H. were located in Berlin, in the Lichterfelde district, where they occupied the former Hauptkadettenanstalt buildings, the most prestigious Prussian officer school.

On August 24, 1939, when Germany was about to start the war, the Führer Begleit Batallion or Escort Battalion was created. It was a military unit charged with ensuring his protection during his travels to the front or on board his armored train. This unit was created from the Grossdeutschland Motorized Infantry Regiment's 7th and 8th companies. In this, it was in keeping with the ancestral tradition of the Stabswatche from the German Empire and Weimar Republic. Colonel Erwin Rommel was originally in command; one of its more famous commanders was Otto Ernst Remer, who was posted in Berlin when Operation *Walkyrie* took place on July 20, 1944. He put a stop to the conspiracy with the aid of the forces he commanded in the capital.

THE FALL

From headquarters to bunkers, Hitler reached Berlin on January 15, 1945. The city was just smoking ruins and became his shroud. For several weeks, to the rhythm of the shelling, the personnel oscillated between the last intact rooms of the new chancellery and the underground bunker. Then, by the end of February, the gray walls of the bunker became the final backdrop for the last of

Hitler's faithful. The Russian bombardments, announced by a sinister "tic-toc" on civilian radio broadcasts, echoed loudly in the concrete, disrupting the steady hum of the ventilation fans. However, if "discipline seemed a little laxer, it still remained strict," remembered Rochus Misch. In the end, it was members of the R.S.D. who would turn the final page of the last act of this tragedy.

A cheque book from the Munich Commerzbank, where the N.S.D.A.P. had its main account, found on Martin Bormann's desk, and showing two payments made on April 14, for an amount nearing 275,000 Reichsmark.

They fulfilled their mission until the end, for the most part following Hitler into death, and the Reich in its fall.

The Red Army was now next door, and many had no illusions as to the fate that awaited them. The fighting in Berlin was of an unheard of brutality and violence.[98]

In this chaos, service carried on, the switchboard was working and staff conferences were proceeding as normal. All clung to the latest news, to the faraway whispers of a possible worn out regiment that could still save Berlin. However, a different wave was crashing in the enclosed space of the bunker: desertions.

A sign of Hitler's closeness with the members of his protection service, it was Heinz Linge who first heard from the Führer's mouth, on April 25, that he had decided to shoot himself in the bunker. In his final instructions, he ordered Linge and his team to cremate his body in the gardens of the chancellery and to destroy all his personal effects. Linge transmitted the Fürher's orders to the other members of the R.S.D. immediately. Högl was specifically put in charge of destroying Hitler's belongings after his suicide.

It was the men of the R.S.D., and more particularly Linge, Günsche and Kempka, who, around 15:30 on April 30, rolled the lifeless bodies of Eva and Adolf Hitler into blankets and took care to cremate them in a bomb crater. As ordered by Hitler, Högl destroyed what was left of his personal belongings; the blood-stained rug was also burned. On all fours, and in vain, they looked for the 7.65mm bullet from the Walter PPK with which Hitler shot

This cap belonged to Sturmbannführer Peter Högl (August 19, 1897–May 2, 1945). Högl was in Berlin in the Führerbunker. On Hitler's orders, Högl arrested SS General Hermann Fegelein as he was trying to flee. On the night of May 2, he was wounded in the head as he was crossing the Weidendamm bridge and died of his wounds.

himself. It was Artur Axmann, the last Reichsjugendleiter of the Hitler Youth, who inherited the weapon.

The discreet bitter almond scent of the prussic acid that Eva Braun took did not distract from the fact that that the Russians were in the gardens, only a grenade-throw away from the armored doors.

Some decided to stay and die in the bunker, others decided to try and escape. Some died before even managing to leave Berlin, like Peter Högl. Others would face more than ten years in Soviet jails, like Linge, Günsche and Rochus Misch.

OTTO GÜNSCHE

Otto Günsche was born in Jena, Thuringia, on September 24, 1917. In 1931, aged 14, he entered the Hitler Youth. He left school in 1933 and started a qualification with view to become a Wehrmacht soldier. He volunteered and integrated the L.S.S.A.H. in August 1934, aged only 17. On March 1, 1935, he joined the Nazi Party. He met Hitler for the first time in 1936, just as he was admitted to the Reichssicherheitsdienst. Between 1940 and 1941, he was part of the Führer's personal guard, as an orderly. He assisted at the signature of the French-German armistice on June 20, 1940, in Compiègne. Later, he studied at the Bad Tölz Military Academy to become an SS officer and served on the eastern front with the L.S.S.A.H. until January 1943.

His height and physique (6'5" for 105 kg) as well as his Germanic looks attracted Hitler's attention, who called him into his service on January 13, 1943. This was how he became the Führer's personal aide-de-camp until August 1943, after which he was called to the front as an Obersturmführer with the 12./Pz.GR.1

Günsche took part in the combats on the Eastern Front as Kompaniechef. He obtained the Iron Cross 1st Class before being named Hitler's aide-de-camp once more, on February 6, 1944. He was present during the *Wolfsschanze* assassination attempt on Hitler, on July 20, 1944. He distinguished himself by helping Hitler out of the rubble, despite being injured himself. The persons present during the explosion received the wounded insignia, personally handed out by the Führer on September 2, 1944.

In January 1945, Hitler moved his headquarters to Berlin and Günsche's duties increased, especially in the Führerbunker. On April 22, Brigadeführer Wilhelm Mohnke took charge of the group in charge of the Reich chancellery's defense. Günsche, at Hitler's request, joined the unit at the side of the remaining Waffen-SS.

On April 27, Hermann Fegelein was accused of desertion and appeared in front of the martial court, who sentenced him to death. It seems Günsche had a role in the decision. Indeed, Hitler had decided to place Fegelein under Brigadeführer Mohnke, until Günsche and Martin Bormann intervened, judging the punishment insufficient to the scale of the crime.

On April 30, with the end of the Third Reich imminent, Hitler personally charged Günsche with disposing of his body after his death. He was also in charge of guarding the entrance of the room where Hitler and Eva Braun committed suicide. He recounted how Magda Goebbels came to see the Führer one last time, to be rejected by him. After waiting 15 minutes, Günsche, Linge and Bormann entered the room, and Günsche announced Hitler's death to the bunker.

They burned the corpses in the chancellery's gardens, with petrol supplied by Erich Kempka. After Hitler's death, Günsche gave Artur Axmann's aide-de-camp, Obersturmbannführer Joachim Hamann, the weapon Hitler used to kill himself. He also took with him a pen that had belonged to Hitler, which he kept all his life.

During the night of May 1, around 22:00, Günsche and his group, led by Wilhelm Mohnke, left the Führerbunker. According to Günsche's description of the events, they managed to escape the chancellery under the bombardment, by going through the U-Bahn in the direction of the Friedrichstrasse and entering the Schultheiss Brewery. There, they learned of Germany's capitulation. At around 18:00 Mohnke, General Joseph Rauch, his orderly and Günsche then decided to negotiate with the Soviets.

On May 2, 1945, Günsche was captured by the Soviet troops that surrounded the city. He was then transferred to the Lubyanka prison, headquarters of the N.K.V.D. in Moscow, with Heinz Linge, to be interrogated by Fyodor Parparov between 1946 and 1949. The methods to extract information concerning Hitler's death were varied. Interrogations took place at night after psychological and physical torture sessions.

Categorized as the "Nation's enemy" and "committed Nazi" by Parparov, Günsche, who was recalcitrant at first, received special treatment. The Soviets wanted their two hostages to confess to Hitler's flight during the Battle of Berlin. The report that came out of these interrogations was handed to Stalin on December 30, 1949. All this was preserved in the Kremlin's archives until 1994, when German historian Matthias Uhl found and published the two Nazi officers' confessions, under the name of *The Hitler Book*.

In 1950, Günsche was sentenced to 25 years of forced labor for war crimes. He spent several years in the Dyaterka camp in the Ural, where he found German ace pilot Erich Hartmann. The book that the latter wrote, *The Blond Knight of Germany*, recounted:

Erich [Hartmann] found himself allied most often with Otto Günsche [... who] proved himself a formidable bruiser if attacked, although otherwise he was a mild and gentle giant. Big, fair-haired and heavy, with brawler's arms and immense strength, Hitler's ex-adjutant was a man of quiet and kindly temperament—the reverse of what might have been expected.

Hartmann also described the Soviet labor camp of Diaterka when he worked there in 1953:

Rows of large barrack buildings, each accommodating from two hundred to four hundred prisoners, provided crude shelter for perhaps four thousand men. The inmates were jammed into three-tier bunks to maximize the capacity of the buildings. [...] Around the buildings, but inside the inner high fence, was a "dead zone" with watchdogs on each side. The inner fence was a ten-footer, crowned with barbed wire. A few yards beyond this was a stockade-type, high wooden fence, with guard points equipped with machine guns at each corner. Beyond the wooden stockade was a barrier of electrified wire. If a man touched it, he could be fried on the spot. Beyond the electrified wire was a final, eight-foot, chain-link fence topped with barbed wire. [...]

The maximum-security pen for problem prisoners [...] was a prison within a prison. [...] Inside were confined some of the Soviet Union's most prized prisoners. [Including] Otto Günsche, Hitler's adjutant for the last two years of the Third Reich.

In 1955, when the majority of German prisoners of war were liberated by the Soviets, Günsche was transferred to the Bautzen prison in East Germany. On May 2, 1956, after Chancellor Konrad Adenauer's visit to Moscow, he was finally freed. He was not subjected to any legal action and went to live in North Rhine-Westphalia, where he worked as administrator in a pharmaceutical company in Cologne.

On October 25, 1956, Otto Günsche and Heinz Linge were summoned to an audience room in Berchtesgaden, by the Munich tribunal to testify about Hitler's presumed death. Their interviews were recorded, and the tapes were re-discovered by Spiegel TV, which restored them and made them public in 2010.

In 1985, he was called to testify once more, regarding Hitler's counterfeit diaries. After this, he managed to stay away from media scrutiny. A widower and father of three children, he never exposed his past as a Nazi officer, refusing interviews with historians, but talking openly on the subject with a small circle of trusted friends. Among the people who were able to garner Günsche's recollections was David Irving, to whom he granted a few interviews from 1967. Furthermore, he often took part in veterans' meetings, like those organized by the H.I.A.G. (Mutual Aid Association for Former Waffen-SS Members).

He died of a heart attack on October 2, 2003, eight days after his 86th birthday, in his home in Lohmar. His body was cremated, and the ashes scattered in the North Sea.

HANS LAMMERS

Hans Lammers was one of those characters that history has forgotten, but who remains one of its important actors. The discovery of the Führerbunker's last telegrams gives us the opportunity to put his role into perspective.

A doctor of law, he was a judge in Silesia in 1912. He volunteered in 1914, earning the Iron Cross. As a committed Nationalist, he joined the D.N.V.P. in 1919 and the N.S.D.A.P. in 1932.

Although he joined rather late, he displayed his allegiance to the party no less professionally. This granted him lightning-fast progress in the career he joined in 1922 at the Internal Affairs Ministry. Lightning-fast is an understatement, as he became in the space of a few years: Counsellor to the Internal Affairs Minister, Secretary of State at the chancellery, then Minister in the same Reich chancellery.

Supported by Frick, Internal Affairs Minister from 1933, he coordinated the government's activities during the first years of the regime. As such, he became a privileged interlocutor between administrative officers, exchanging numerous correspondence, and establishing the jurisdiction and relationship between the Third Reich's main power centers.

On November 26, 1937, whilst keeping his privileges, he was named minister without portfolio, and became de facto the Reich's main administrator. Taking advantage of Hitler's detachment from current affairs, he took decisions that should have been the government's responsibility, for example when, in 1938, a woman was named assistant master at the Berlin University. As State Secretary at the Reich chancellery, he was responsible for the coordination of ministerial work, but from 1934, his remit was intertwined with the institutional tangles of the Reich.

He promptly proved himself the only man able to coordinate the various ministers and guarantee interaction with the Chancellor. Thus, responsible for the enforcement of legislative and regulatory texts, he had to give instructions to the Reich's governors, whilst the latter, often Gauleiters, took their orders from the competent authorities of the N.S.D.A.P., or the Prussian Internal Affairs Minister.

In his line of work, he was often called to communicate the Führer's point of view, through circulars addressed to civil servants. His ministerial colleagues also communicated with him as he disseminated Hitler's opinions or as he coordinated the actions of those parts of the administration for which he was responsible.

Finally, Lammers was also the civil servants' interlocutor and representative when the regime took decisions that concerned them. At first, he alone controlled access to the Reich's Chancellor; apart from a few exceptions, all interview requests had to go through him. As time went on though, he had to share his powers with Hess, Bormann and others. Similarly, he had to coordinate the chancellery's activities from its various sections, especially when it was dealing with particular cases.

He decided which of those files presented to him were passed on to the Chancellor (or buried), and if so when and how to do it, influencing Hitler's decisions. As years went by, he tried to become the main guarantor of the state's power against the N.S.D.A.P., opposing in particular after the Nuremberg Rally, the domination of the N.S.D.A.P. over the state.

During his service to the Reich chancellery, he took part in the multiple power struggles that peppered the government of the Reich by the N.S.D.A.P., seeming less and less like a neutral referee. In these fights for power, he always looked for support before presenting even the least text to Hitler for signing.

However, he did retain until late in the conflict, real responsibilities for the organization of the work of government. Responsible for the coordination of the disgrace of some of Hitler's close supporters, he was not merely a witness, but also the man responsible for giving this a legal basis.

In time, in the context of the ever increasing overlap of the functions of the central State, the N.S.D.A.P. and various specific organs of state, his responsibilities, as well as his power, evolved. This evolution culminated, in the last year of the Third Reich, in him being ousted in favor of Bormann.

From the time of Rudolf Hess' capture in 1941, he had to work with his successor Martin Bormann, named Chief of the Party Chancellery on April 12, 1941. From August 12, 1942, at Bormann's request, he was obliged to give the latter all the files requiring Hitler's opinion, as he was "not present." On June 17, 1943, the two men, who were on first name terms, found a solution that served the interests of the government best: Bormann agreed to take Lammers with him during discussions with Hitler concerning the Reich's government.

But as months went by, he saw himself increasingly excluded from the Chancellor's presence by Bormann, who also seized his role as ministry coordinator in the last two years of the conflict.

As a consequence of Bormann's rise in power, his exclusion appeared complete by the middle of 1944; the Party's chancellery, Bormann's domain, having completely eclipsed the Reich's chancellery and government.

During the last months of the conflict, completely discarded, he suffered from depression and was unable to exercise his now redundant functions. So it was that, in March 1945, on the pretext of his health, he left Berlin to take refuge in Berchtesgaden, whilst the Reich chancellery was entrusted to his deputy.

He was sentenced by the Allied tribunal at the ministers' trial, to twenty years in prison, reduced to ten in 1951. He was freed on December 16, 1951 and died in Düsseldorf on January 4, 1962.

Epilogue

IN THE 1980S, REPORTER BRUNO Renoult, who lived in West Berlin, was regularly crossing the wall to visit its eastern zone, then the D.D.R.'s capital. From 1985, Honecker's government decided to destroy the last vestiges of the bunker and the Führer's chancellery. Weekly explosions shook Berlin's heart on the other side of the wall. In 1987, the historian decided to see it for himself. He found a huge site; the whole sector had become a huge quarry. Both Führerbunkers had been revealed, the Vorbunker was being eaten by massive machines and dynamite. The work was considerable, and the huge underground system of the chancellery was being revealed. But how to access this site heavily guarded by the Volkspolizei?

Having parked his car on a side street, the reporter took a hard hat from the site, a roll of paper, and managed to enter the site by pretending to be a harassed foreman. Making his way through the diggers, he took photographs of the ruins, the bunker itself and the remains of the bunker's exit stairway, where Hitler's body was taken to be burned. The building was already heavily damaged by the explosions, rubble showing through 50 cm of water. But the underground passages leading from the bunker to the chancellery's cellars were sill recognizable, and the cellars themselves still intact: boiler room, vaults, hospital, etc.

He took some souvenirs, pieces of the red marble that decorated the chancellery, tiles, switches and ventilation parts, the whole lot in a cement bag. Coming out of the site, he was intercepted by a foreman: "What are you doing here?"

"Oh, I'm a bit of an archaeologist, I'm taking a few souvenirs." "Go now and leave everything you took behind!" But, understanding that he was French and a little amused by his actions, the foreman struck up a conversation, and told him that some objects had been found that he could give him in exchange for some West Marks. He came back after a brief moment, with a silver sugar bowl, engraved with the Eagle and Hitler's monogram A.H. Not pushing his luck, the reporter took everything to his car and passed back through the wall. At Checkpoint Charlie, a Volkspolizei wondered at the rubble and scrap in his trunk. "Oh, I just forgot to empty my trunk before leaving Paris…"

In 1990, the bunker of the chancellery's chauffeurs was discovered nearby, at the same time the wall was being taken down. An opportunity for Bruno Renoult to make another report.

Endnotes

1   Martin Kitchen, *Speer: Hitler's Architect*. Yale University Press, 2017, p. 41.

2   "A day with Hitler" by André Beucler, *Le Petit Parisien*, Thursday October 5, 1933.

3   The initial budget of 28 million Reichsmark was widely underestimated and by the end, reached over 70 million.

4   Georges Bernage, *Berlin 1945, l'Agonie du Reich*, Heimdal, 2009, p. 6.

5   M. Hitler inaugure la nouvelle chancellerie, *L'Homme Libre*, Tuesday January 10, 1939.

6   La Nouvelle Chancellerie du Reich. *Le Monde Illustré, Miroir du Monde*, January 21, 1939.

7   Thomas Fischer, *Berlin 1933–45 avec Wilhelm Mohnke*, Heimdal, 2013, pp. 21–22.

8   George Bernage, Op. cit., p. 49.

9   Christa Schröder, *12 ans auprès d'Hitler, 1933–1945. La Secrétaire Privée d'Hitler Témoigne*. Editions Page Après Page, 2004, p. 143.

10 Traudl Junge, *Until the Final Hour: Hitler's Last Secretary*, Arcade Publishing, 2003.

11 Patrick Fleuridas, *Au coeur de la Chancellerie, le Führerbunker, Histomag 39–45*, n° 93, November 2015–January 2016, p. 139.

12 *12 Ans Auprès d'Hitler*, Op. cit., p. 147.

13 According to Wilhelm Monke: "When I went to down to see Hitler... from the *Vorbunker*, located higher up, I had to go down in the deeper *Hauptbunker*, the real *Führerbunker*, by two spiral staircases. I can still remember clearly that there were first four steps, and then a 90° angle, and another four steps. Such insignificant details deeply mark one's memory! In any case, I felt much more at ease at my command post under the Chancellery. One was always happy to leave the *Führerbunker*." Quoted from Thomas Fischer, Op. cit., p. 45.

14 Rochus Misch, *J'étais garde du corps d'Hitler, 1940–1945*, Testimony gathered by Nicolas Bourcier, Le Cherche Midi, 2006.

15 Thomas Fischer, Op. cit., p. 44.

16 Ibid.

17 *12 ans auprès d'Hitler*, Op. cit., pp. 149–150.

18 From what we know, Bormann set up residence in the Chancellery's bunker around February 2, 1945, when a room was allocated to him.

19 Quoted from Georges Bernage, "Berlin 1945" *39–45 Magazine*, Hors-série Historica, n° 82, January–February–March 2005, p. 80.

20 Armin D. Lehmann, Tim Carroll, *In Hitler's Bunker: A Boy Soldier's Eyewitness Account of the Führer's Last Days*, Mainstream Publishing, 2003.

21 Joachim Fest, *Inside Hitler's Bunker: The Last Days of the Third Reich*, 2004, Farrar Straus Giroux.

22 Quoted by Henri Fenet, *Berlin: Derniers Témoignages*, Éditions de l'Homme Libre, 2014, p. 84.

23 Ibid, p. 85.

24 Rochus Misch, Op. Cit.

25 According to his valet Heinz Linge, Hitler sometimes got up around 14:00, after falling asleep at dawn and having eaten a few slices of cake.

26 Rochus Misch, Op. cit.

27 André Besson, *Les 30 jours de Berlin. 8 avril–8 mai 1945,* France-Empire, 1985.

28 Thomas Fischer, Op. cit., p. 48.

29 Quoted from Mario Frank, *Hitler, la chute. Dans le Bunker Heure par Heure,* Presses de la Cité, 2008, p. 81.

30 Quoted from Pierre Galante and Eugène Silianoff, *Les Derniers Témoins du Bunker,* Filipacchi, 1989, pp. 211–212.

31 Armin D. Lehmann, Tim Carroll, Op. cit.

32 Bernd Freytag von Loringhoven with François d'Alançon, *In the Bunker with Hitler: The Last Witness Speaks*, Phoenix, 2006.

33 Quoted from Henri Fenet, Op. cit., p. 74.

34 The avenues running between the Brandenburg Gate and the Victory Column were used as a landing and take-off strip in the last days of Berlin's encirclement.

35 Pierre Galante and Eugène Silianoff, Op. cit., pp. 223–224.

36 Bernd Freytag von Loringhoven, Op. cit.

37 Thomas Fischer, Op. cit., pp. 58–59.

38 Ibid, p. 59.

39 Rochus Misch, Op. cit.

40 Armin Lehmann, Tim Carroll, Op. cit.

41 Henri Fenet, Op. cit., p. 81.

42 Rochus Misch, Op. cit.

43 Quoted from Armin Lehmann, Tim Carroll, Op. cit.

44 Ibid.

45 Quoted from Henri Fenet, Op. cit., p. 84.

46 Quoted from Thomas Fischer, Op. cit., pp. 71–73.

47 Quoted from Ibid, p. 71.

48 James P. O'Donnell, *The Bunker*, Da Capo Press, 2001 (re-edition), p. 424.

49 Quoted from Anne Wiazemsky, *My Berlin Child*, Europa Editions, 2011, p. 256.

50 Ibid.

51 Ibid.

52 It was Luftwaffe General Köller who was at that meeting and told Army General Jodl, who in turn confided in Luftwaffe General Christian, who took the news to Göring.

53 Raoul Nordling, born in Paris on November 11, 1882 and died on October 1, 1962 in Neuilly-sur-Seine, was a businessman and Swedish Consul and played an important role in the liberation of Paris in August 1944.

54   Hitler's aide-de-camp in the Luftwaffe.

55   *Reichssicherheitsdienst* (R.S.D.), or the Reich's Security Service, was a security force of the Third Reich responsible for Adolf Hitler's protection, as well as—in the final years—that of senior Nazi dignitaries.

56   SS-Obersturmbannführer (lieutenant-colonel) Wilhelm Bredow (30.12.1914 in Brême–?) was a member of the SS-Kommando Obersalzberg.

57   Bernhard Frank (1913–2011) was a SS Obersturmbannführer. He was the last Commander of the SS Obersalzberg guard and wrote his autobiography and gave many interviews after the war.

58   Karl Köller (1898–1951) was a general and the last Chief of Staff of the Luftwaffe.

59   Karl Zenger (4.11.1904–?) was a non-commissioned SS officer. A member of the Obersalzberg R.S.D., this position afforded him the function of *Kriminalobersecretär* (criminal police secretary).

60   Lammer's orderly.

61   Gerhard Klopfer (1905–1987) was born in Schreibersdorf in Prussian Silesia (today in Poland). After studying Law and Economics, he became a judge in Düsseldorf in 1931. When the Nazis came to power in 1933, He joined the N.S.D.A.P. and the SA, and in 1934 joined the Gestapo. In 1935, he joined Rudolf Hess' team and the SS with the rank Oberführer. By 1938, he was in charge of seizing Jewish properties, "mixed marriages" between Germans and Jews, and general matters regarding the occupation of foreign states. As the State Secretary of the Party's chancellery, he represented Martin Bormann, leading the N.S.D.A.P. chancellery. In 1945, Klopfer was captured and accused of war crimes, but was later released due to a lack of proof. He became a tax advisor in Ulm (Baden-Wurtemberg). He later settled in Fairfax, Virginia.

62   Occupied since April 9, 1940, it would only be freed on May 8, 1945, after the German capitulation.

63   Also liberated on May 8, 1945.

64   This Army Group was created on January 24, 1945 to protect Berlin from the Soviet armies that were advancing from the River Vistula. Early on in its formation, it was noted that the name was poorly chosen as most units were concentrated east of the Oder.

65   Heeresgruppe Kurland was a group of Wehrmacht armies during World War II. It was created on the Eastern Front from the remains of the Army Group North, isolated in the Courland peninsula by the Soviet troops' advance during the Baltic offensive in 1944. This group remained isolated there until May 8, 1945. All units received the order to capitulate from the Wehrmacht, which amounted to 180,000 men.

66   Walter Wenck (1900–1982) was the youngest of the German generals.

67   Karl Jesko von Puttkamer (1900–1981) was a German admiral, Hitler's deputy in the Navy. He left Berlin in the night of April 22 to take refuge in Berchtesgaden with many of Hitler's closest followers.

68   Führerbau was one of the buildings of the N.S.D.A.P.'s central administration in Munich. It still stands today. This was where the Munich agreement was signed in 1938.

69 Wilhelm Zander (April 22, 1911–September 27, 1974), born in Munich, was Bormann's orderly during World War II.

70 Heinrich Walkenhorst was one of Bormann's deputies and an important member of the N.S.D.A.P.

71 Codename for one of the Heer's generals supposed to free Berlin.

72 Paul Giesler, born June 15, 1895 and deceased May 8, 1945, was a member of the N.S.D.A.P., he was the South Westphalia Gauleiter (Westfalen-Süd) from 1941 to 1942, then a Gauleiter, München-Oberbayern from April 12, 1944 to May 1945. He was also Bavaria's Ministerpräsident from November 2, 1942 to April 28, 1945, at which time Hitler named him Interior Minister of the Reich. A title which he kept a few days, in the ephemeral government of Flensbourg led by Karl Dönitz, before committing suicide with his wife in Berchtesgaden, on the last day of the conflict.

73 The *Reichsverteidigungskommissar* (R.V.K.), was the Reich's Defense Commissioner. It was a position created by decree on September 1, 1939 and exclusively given to Gauleiters. The R.V.K.s had a defensive function, including the direction of units from all civilian administration branches. They had authority in matters of defense, public services, air raid protection and over refugee populations. The concept of "total war" decided by Goebbels drastically increased their powers.

74 Friedrich Wilhelm Kritzinger (born April 4, 1890 in Grünfier, died April 25, 1947, Nuremberg) was a German politician, second in command of the Reich Chancellery led by Hans Lammers. In May 1945, he was, as Secretary of State, part of Karl Dönitz's ephemeral government. Arrested in 1946, he was later acquitted and died in Nuremberg.

75 Abbreviation for *Parteigenosse*, party member.

76 *SS-Obergruppenführer* Ernst Kaltenbrunner, born October 4, 1903 in Ried im Innkreis, Austria, was one of the main actors of the Nazi police system. During the Nuremberg trials, he was sentenced to death for war crimes and crimes against humanity, and was hanged in Nuremberg on October 16, 1946.

77 This could be Herbert Backe. Born on May 1, 1896, Backe was a German politician, Secretary of the State for Agriculture from 1933 to 1942, then Minister for Food from 1942 until the Flensburg government's dissolution on May 23, 1945. He was considered one of the authors of the "Famine Plan." In the last days of the conflict, in the early spring of 1945, he tried to see to the most pressing needs, and attempted to supply Berlin with enough food to avoid a crisis whilst also organizing an emergency program for the production of agricultural materials. Captured by the Allies at the end of the war, he committed suicide on April 6, 1947, hanging himself in his cell in Nuremberg.

78 Hans Briegel (1906–1988) was a Major in the paratroopers of the Hermann Göring Regiment. He was one of the last soldiers to be allocated the Iron Cross on January 14, 1945.

79 Franz Budka (1920–1945) was a junior officer of SS Festungs-Regiment 1 Besslein. He was one of the last soldiers to be allocated the Iron Cross on April 19, 1945. An improvised regiment formed in February 1945 to defend Breslau, they held out for 82 days and finally surrendered on May 6, 1945. Only two men were decorated with the Knight's Cross: SS-Obersturmbannführer Georg-Robert Besslein, the regiment's creator, and second lieutenant Budka.

80 Georg von Unold (1905–1946) was a colonel in the 252nd Infantry Division. His division fought in Poland in April 1945. He died in captivity in a Russian prisoner-of-war camp. He already held the Knight's Cross of the Iron Cross from March 20, 1945.

81 Wilhelm Burgdorf (born February 14, 1895 and deceased May 1, 1945) was a German general who was also Hitler's senior aide-de-camp during the last month of the conflict. It was he who brought Rommel the news of his death sentence and handed him the cyanide pill. Burgdorf committed suicide in the bunker on May 1, 1945.

82 Hitler's Luftwaffe aide-de-camp.

83 The transport corps of the N.S.D.A.P.

84 Louis-Carl Bruno Heroux (1868–1944), German painter, engraver and illustrator.

85 Ilse Bormann, nicknamed Eicke (1931–1957) was said to resemble her father, as much physically as mentally. She died suddenly, aged 26 after marrying an Italian engineer.

86 The Mother's Cross of Honor (*Ehrenkreuz der Deutschen Mutter*) or more simply Mother's Cross (*Mutterkreuz*) was a state medal given by the Third Reich. Created on December 16, 1938, this decoration distinguished the excellence of some German mothers. Originally reserved to native Germans, it was increasingly given to Austrians and Sudeten Germans. There were three orders, bronze, silver and gold. The first recipient was decorated on May 21, 1939 and the decoration disappeared with the Third Reich on May 8, 1945. Magda Goebbels, wife of Propaganda Minister Joseph Goebbels, was first to receive this medal.

87 Otto Günsche (1917–2003) was an SS officer. Member of Hitler's personal guard, then of the R.S.D. (*Reichssicherheitsdienst*) charged with his personal protection, he was Hitler's last aide-de-camp. He was charged by Hitler to take care of his and Eva Braun's bodies after their suicide (see chapters 1 to 6).

88 The Freikorps (Free Corps), were volunteer armies which formed in the German Empire and evolved in the Baltic countries at the end of World War I. Composed of demobilized soldiers after the German defeat, they were part of numerous paramilitary groups during the Weimar Republic.

89 Gerhard Rossbach was born on February 28, 1893 in Kehrberg. Member of the Nazi Party, Rossbach took part in the Beer Hall Putsch in 1923. He was recruited later by Adolf Hitler to develop the SA organization. He fell out with Hitler when he came to power in January 1933 and was arrested in 1934 during the Night of the Long Knives. Historian Robert G. L. Waite described Rossbach as a sadistic murderer and known homosexual. He died on August 30, 1967.

90 Albert Leo Schlageter, born in Schönau im Schwarzwald (Bade) on August 12, 1894, was a German fighter in the Freikorps, considered a martyr during the Weimar Republic, which above all helped the propaganda at the beginning of the Third Reich. He died on the Golzheimer plain near Düsseldorf on May 26, 1923.

91 Baldur von Schirach, *J'ai cru en Hitler*, Plon, 1968, p. 212.

92 Antony Beevor, *Berlin: The Downfall, 1945,* Op. cit., chapter 14.

93 Born on November 24, 1891 in Munich, Amann fought in World War I as a Sergeant. Corporal Adolf Hitler who was under his command, was recommended for promotion to the rank of Unteroffizier. He registered with the N.S.D.A.P. on October 1, 1921. In 1922,

he was named Director of the Eher-Verlag publishing company. He took part in the Beer Hall Putsch in November 1923 and was imprisoned with Adolf Hitler in Landsberg. In 1933, he became president of Reich Media Chamber (*Reichspressekammer*), which depended on Joseph Goebbels. Arrested by Allied troops at the end of World War II, Amann was sentenced on September 8, 1948 to ten years of forced labor but was only freed in 1953. Deprived of his belongings and his right to pension, he died in poverty in Munich on March 30, 1957.

94 It was in front of this building that the November 9, 1923 putsch failed, resulting in the death of 16 National Socialists.

95 When Hitler visited Austria, the R.S.D. assembled 10 officers, 31 men armed with 14 Machine pistols, 2,596 rounds, each man had two pistols, whilst the Führer's Adjutant had two Machine pistols. His cars were equipped too, including Mauser Schnellfeuers placed in compartments in the doors.

96 Indeed, Linge, his valet, was a member of the R.S.D., just like Kempka, his chauffeur. Both remained by his side until the end.

97 Heinz Linge's memoirs' title is revealing: *Bis zu Ende* (Until the End).

98 The Battle of Berlin (April 16–May 2, 1945) killed or wounded 458,000 Germans and 81,116 Soviets. Two million civilians were trapped in the city, which was destroyed up to 70 percent in the center. 100,000 Berliner women were raped by Russian troops.

Index